THE USE OF "DESIGN" IN A MANAGEMENT SENSE GOES BEYOND THE PHYSICAL ENVIRONMENT TO AN ORDERING OF RELATIONSHIPS THAT ENCOURAGE CREATIVITY AND COOPERATION THAT BENEFITS THE ORGANIZATION.

RICHARD SWETT

I TRULY BELIEVE THAT MANY ORGANIZATIONS DESIRE TO CREATE BETTER WORKPLACES. THE REASON THEY FAIL IS THAT THEY DON'T KNOW HOW.

DANIEL PINK

CONSIDER THE ENORMOUS POPULARITY AND ENDURANCE OF THE DILBERT-LIKE CUBICLE. WAS THERE EVER A DESIGN SO SUPERFICIALLY FUNCTIONAL AND YET UTTERLY SOULLESS?

JEANNE LIEDTKA

WE KNOW INTUITIVELY THAT ENVIRONMENT IMPACTS PEOPLE'S BEHAVIOR—THEIR MOODS AND PRODUCTIVITY. THE MOST SUCCESSFUL ORGANIZATIONS TODAY ARE LEARNING TO TRUST THAT INTUITION.

SCOTT WYATT

AN ENVIRONMENT IS TALKING ALL THE TIME.
AND A LOT OF THAT TALKING — NOT
ONLY IN ENVIRONMENTS BUT IN COMPANIES
GENERALLY — IS MUMBLING AND GRUMBLING
AND WHISPERED COMPLAINTS.

BRUCE MAU

DESIGN IS A CUSTOM BUSINESS,
NOT A SIGNATURE BUSINESS — IF THERE IS A SIGNATURE
ON A BUILDING, IT'S THE COMPANY'S SIGNATURE.

SCOTT WYATT

THE DESIRE FOR FLEXIBILITY OFTEN
TAKES THE EASY WAY OUT, SETTLING FOR BLAND
SPACES THAT GIVE LITTLE THOUGHT
TO ANY ONE PURPOSE IN THEIR RUSH
TO ACCOMMODATE MANY PURPOSES.
THE SPECIFICITY THAT MAKES GREAT DESIGN
SO ENGAGING IS SACRIFICED. DESIGNS
ENDURE WHEN THEY GET THE BASICS — THE
UNDERSTANDING OF A PARTICULAR SET OF
HUMAN NEEDS AND WANTS — RIGHT.

JEANNE LIEDTKA

An honest image. It is the

THE OFFICE BUILDING IS THE ARK IN WHICH
MOST BUSINESS SAILS. GOOD MANAGERS UNDERSTAND
THEIR BUILDING; THEY EXCEL IF IT SUPPORTS
THE WAY THEY WANT THEIR FIRM TO FUNCTION, IF IT
HELPS PEOPLE TO COMMUNICATE, IF IT PRESENTS
CUSTOMERS THE RIGHT IMAGE. THEY KNOW THEY HAVE
A COMPETITIVE ADVANTAGE IF THEIR BUILDING
PERFORMS BETTER THAN THE NORM.

ALEXI MARMOT

IN THE PAST CENTURY ARCHITECTURE HAS
BEEN CONCEIVED OF AS "HARDWARE"—THE PHYSICAL,
MATERIAL, FIXED PART OF AN OPERATING SYSTEM.
WHAT WE NOW KNOW IS THAT ARCHITECTURE
ISN'T HARDWARE; IT'S SOFTWARE. IT'S A SOFTWARE
PLATFORM THAT SUPPORTS APPLICATIONS.

BRUCE MAU

NOT MANY COMPANIES ARE SAYING, "WE WANT TO BE
THE SAME FOR THE REST OF TIME." MOST COMPANIES HAVE
TREMENDOUS NEEDS FOR CHANGE. IF YOU BUILD
A BUILDING AROUND A COMPANY'S EXISTING PROGRAM,
YOU'VE MISSED THE REAL OPPORTUNITY.

SCOTT WYATT

THE OPPORTUNITY IS TO TAKE A
BUILDING'S MESSAGE AND TO MAKE IT A SONG,
TO MAKE IT SING ABOUT VALUE AND
POTENTIAL AND POSSIBILITIES.

BRUCE MAU

Östberg Library of Design Management

ISBN-10: 0-9755654-6-X
ISBN-13: 978-0-9755654-6-9

Book design: Bruce Mau Design Inc.

Printed by: Bowne of Canada

Published by: Greenway Communications, LLC, a division
of The Greenway Group, 25 Technology Parkway South,
Suite 101, Atlanta, GA 30092 1 800.726.8603

www.greenway.us

CHANGE DESIGN

CONVERSATIONS ABOUT ARCHITECTURE AS THE ULTIMATE BUSINESS TOOL

TO RICK BUCKLEY

A discussion is growing in the business and design worlds. Businesses are creating Chief Design Officers. Business schools are introducing design programs. Business magazines are launching design and innovation channels online. In all these venues, the critical role of design in business is the hot topic of talk.

In this talk, there's a new value placed on design innovation and design solutions. When they're successful, these solutions forgo predictable answers in favor of transformational results and collaborative partnerships.

These new ways of working are critical because so many public and private sector organizations are embarking on building projects in an environment of change—whether change in market, in technology, in mission, in strategy, in structure, or in operations. Rather than trying to mitigate change, many enterprises are responding by redesigning their physical environments to purposefully encourage and accomplish change.

NBBJ has launched an initiative called Change Design. Its purpose is to explore new directions, tools, and methodologies used to develop environments that are performance-driven, humanistic, and sustainable. This book is the first expression of that exploration. It is the result of a series of conversations, workshops, brainstorming sessions, and panel discussions, and its structure reflects that. The book is organized around four major elements: Change Design Conversations, Change Design Talking Points, Change Design Essays, and Change Tools.

CHANGE DESIGN CONVERSATIONS

Seven visionary leaders of prominent corporations, leading educational organizations, key governmental structures, and top research institutions share their insights on using design as a tool for cultural change. In their own words, the leaders talk openly about the ambitions, risks, hurdles, and accomplishments of their "change design" projects.

The common thread in these interviews is the synergy between business and design, a synergy that has relaunched each enterprise's unique potential. Each enterprise has used design to ensure that its physical environment reflects a long view of its needs, not just the first use that is identifiable now. Each enterprise has recognized that a physical environment is more than a fixed place; it is also a flexible program.

CHANGE DESIGN TALKING POINTS

To illustrate how change design is used in different ways, the long-form conversations are interspersed with six snapshots of enterprises that have used or are using design to enact a wide variety of changes. These snapshots highlight the talking points of each project, whether it's a corporate headquarters that links people and mission; a residential high-rise that reenergizes a city; an office building that rebrands a neighborhood; or a hospital expansion that reorients a healthcare practice.

In contrast to the Change Design Conversations, which are focused on built projects, the Change Design Talking Points offer glimpses into projects at all phases, from long-built and proven, to just-built and being tested, to designed and under construction.

CHANGE DESIGN ESSAYS

To link this book to that wider conversation, Change Design invited a group of writers, consultants, academics, and designers who have been thinking about design and business to a round table conducted by email. Participants included author Daniel Pink; architect and former US ambassador Richard Swett; workplace consultant Alexi Marmot; and business school professor Jeanne Liedtka. Their thinking, along with that of Bruce Mau Design's Creative Director, Bruce Mau, is captured here in a series of one-page Change Design Essays.

CHANGE TOOLS

To help clients use architectural design to encourage and accomplish change, NBBJ has developed and adopted certain methods, or tools, that are not part of the traditional architectural tool box. Over the course of many projects, NBBJ has discovered that by using these "change tools" in concert with the traditional architectural tools it is possible to design buildings that transform the way enterprises of all sorts work.

Change tools are intended to enable clients and design teams to address issues of change across multiple dimensions: behavioral, relational, organizational, and performance related. The tools in this book represent a cross section of a greater tool box that NBBJ uses to help its clients, its designers and others envision, work together, reach common understanding, and get things done.

The tools are described at the back of this book, in a section called Change Tools. They are also illustrated as anecdotes within the Change Design Conversations. If the tool descriptions are useful and the tool stories illuminating, then this book will have achieved its ambition: to be itself a tool for Change Design.

CONTENTS

CONTENTS

NO PAPER,
NO OFFICE,
NO PROBLEM.

Telenor CEO Jon Fredrik Baksaas transformed his public
monopoly into a competitive multinational by canceling
cubicles, losing land lines, and creating a collaborative
workforce on the banks of a Norwegian fjord.

TELENOR IS NORWAY'S LARGEST TELECOMMUNICATIONS PROVIDER, WITH 2.7 MILLION MOBILE SUBSCRIPTIONS AND 2.3 MILLION FIXED PHONE LINES AND ISDN SUBSCRIPTIONS. OUTSIDE NORWAY, TELENOR SERVES MORE THAN 75 MILLION MOBILE SUBSCRIBERS THROUGH ITS OWNERSHIP STAKES IN 11 INTERNATIONAL MOBILE OPERATORS. TELENOR ALSO SERVES 2.7 MILLION SATELLITE AND CABLE-BASED TV SUBSCRIBERS.

TELENOR CONSOLIDATED 40 BUILDINGS IN THE OSLO AREA INTO A NEW WATERFRONT HEADQUARTERS BUILT ON THE MAIN RUNWAY OF FORNEBU, THE CITY'S FORMER INTERNATIONAL AIRPORT ON OSLO FJORD.

TWO CRESCENT-SHAPED BUILDINGS HOUSE EIGHT OFFICE WINGS, EACH WITH ITS OWN ATRIUM. EMPLOYEES ARE ASSIGNED TO ONE OF 200 WORK ZONES ACCOMMODATING 40 PEOPLE EACH.

AT 1.5 MILLION SQUARE FEET (137,000 SQUARE METERS) TELENOR'S NEW CAMPUS IS THE BIGGEST CORPORATE HEADQUARTERS IN THE NORDIC REGION. DESPITE ITS SIZE, THE NEW CAMPUS HAS REDUCED THE AMOUNT OF SPACE THE COMPANY OCCUPIES BY 40 PERCENT AND CUT ITS ANNUAL OPERATING COSTS BY $3 MILLION.

THE BUILDING IS THE WORLD'S LARGEST IMPLEMENTATION OF "HOT DESKING"— WHERE EMPLOYEES DO NOT HAVE DEDICATED WORKSPACES. THE HEADQUARTERS CAN CATER TO 7,500 EMPLOYEES SHARING 6,000 WORKSTATIONS, 225 MEETING ROOMS, 40 VIDEO CONFERENCING SITES, FOUR RESTAURANTS, AND THREE COFFEE BARS.

THE BUILDING HAS ONE OF EUROPE'S LARGEST WIRELESS LOCAL AREA NETWORKS, WITH 32,000 PORTS FOR PHONE AND DATA EXCHANGE.

IT IS A PAPER-FREE ENVIRONMENT. MAILROOMS SCAN PRINTED DOCUMENTS, SEND THE ELECTRONIC FILES TO RECIPIENTS, THEN SHRED AND RECYCLE THE PAPER. MEETING ROOM ELECTRONIC WHITEBOARDS CONVERT MEETING NOTES TO ELECTRONIC FILES.

JON FREDRIK BAKSAAS
PRESIDENT AND CEO, TELENOR

Jon Fredrik Baksaas has been President and CEO of Telenor since June 2002. He is in charge of the day-to-day management of operations at Telenor ASA and in the Telenor Group. He joined Telenor in 1989 and was made Deputy CEO in 1997. Baksaas has held positions as Finance Director, Executive Vice President, and CEO of TBK AS, a subsidiary specializing in system integration. Before joining Telenor, Baksaas held finance-related positions in Aker AS, Stolt-Nielsen Seaway and Det Norske Veritas. He is a board member of Svenska Handelsbanken AB. Baksaas holds a Master of Science in Business Administration from the Norwegian School of Economics and Business Administration in Bergen and has additional qualifications from IMD in Lausanne, Switzerland.

Describe your own workspace at Telenor's new Fornebu headquarters. What does it look like? We made a point of standardizing all workstations, so as the CEO of Telenor I have the same type of workstation as all my colleagues. We have an open space area for about 15 people called the Group Management Area. This open area facilitates easy communication and information sharing between the different group managers. On the other side of the coin, we make sure we maintain a versatile area where we can concentrate and work in more silent modes.

Let's go back to when you first started to plan for this new headquarters. Telenor was at a turning point. Can you tell me how the company was changing? In the mid '90s the telecommunication industry in Europe was undergoing a lot of changes. Competition was the target in all markets, and liberalization was taking place at high speed. Several licenses—particularly in the mobile field—were issued for the national market, and Telenor had to prepare to move from a monopoly situation into a competitive situation. And we did that in two ways. We started to prepare ourselves for the new market conditions in Norway, and we started an international program where we took our competencies into other markets.

You could say that having been a monopoly operation for quite a number of years—we celebrated our 150th anniversary in 2005—getting competitors in the domestic market was quite a change. This moves the core competencies of the group—over a long period of time, of course—from being very technology-focused to becoming a more customer-oriented company. And this change was stimulated by also co-locating all our activities into a brand-new headquarters building.

You had 40 buildings scattered throughout Oslo? Yes, we had more than 40 different addresses around Oslo, approximately 250,000 square meters altogether. At that point in time, we also had a fair amount of leasing contracts, which made it easier for us to take the step of moving into a headquarters, which we took responsibility for ourselves.

So, we were very deliberate in our co-location efforts in order to build a business culture around the co-location exercise, and in hindsight it has worked in a tremendous way.

CHANGE TOOL IN ACTION: 03
KEEP YOUR EYES ON THE PRIZE
As you approach the campus, or see it from the fjord, it looks like a hill town. It's not an iconic building from the outside, purposefully. It looks and acts like an assemblage of little buildings, spaces, offices, and courtyards — a community.

You discover the expression of their vision inside. It's the big plaza. Significant plazas have always been significant historically. In Norway they're important spaces because Norwegians love to be outside, due to the long, dark winters. There are more outdoor seats in Oslo's restaurants, per capita, than in any other city of the world. They celebrate being outside.

So the expression and organization, rather than being outward facing and of a singular nature, is of two embracing, sweeping arms that form a central courtyard encouraging interaction and exchange.

BILL NICHOLS
Partner, NBBJ

Would you say the main role that a new building could play in meeting the challenges the company faced was in creating a new culture? Well, the different communication platforms lived in separate silos. The mobile guys lived in one building, the fixed guys lived in a second building, the TV guys lived in a third building, and from there you could go on.

And all these operations were, in a way, fully set up, independent companies, with their own reception, security measures, server platforms, and so on. We organized the co-location efforts in such a way that we could very easily spot and recognize double work functions; we made people visible to each other in a completely new fashion. And here comes the architecture and gives a helping hand in facilitating communication across business units in a very attentive way.

When you launched the competition to find designers for the building, you said — and you were very explicit about this — that your ambition was to create Scandinavia's leading workplace for innovative activities. What did you have in mind? We were of the opinion that the traditional way — at least, what we felt we had in our history — was that people were working in very closed environments, in closed groups. And as a manager, at that point in time, we had to spend a lot of energy getting one core competence to play with another core competence in another company. We were of the opinion that if we could let these groups meet each other, in a more easy physical atmosphere, it would generate new ideas, reduce time to market, and increase Telenor's ability to keep pace with the general market developments in the telecommunications area.

You had seven design firms on the competition short list. Of the schemes presented — why did you pick this one? The final concept that we decided to go for was called the Uffizi. The Uffizi is a palace, designed by an Italian architect back in the 16th century, I think. The team called it the Uffizi in the Wall meaning that two buildings were, in a way, mirrored towards each other, creating a plaza in between them, and with this approach we could maintain separation between business areas. At the same time we could create an arena where people could meet easily, and there were very small distances from one unit to another.

I think we really achieved that, and if there is something that our employees

are very satisfied with these days it is that it is easy to meet, it is easy to exchange views, it's done in an informal way, and the number of formal meetings has decreased quite significantly.

But it requires that we, from a management point of view, really put people together so that they increase their knowledge about each other, professional as well as personal.

As a technology company you have an opportunity to be ahead of the technology curve. How did you believe that technology was going to change the way work was done, and how did your new building need to respond to the changes that you were anticipating? From a technology point of view, we in this building were the first ones in the Nordic countries to integrate mobile services and PC data connections in the same package. As an example, we made it so that all employees moved to mobile phones as their communication medium.

Are there any land lines? I'm talking to you on the land line in a meeting room today. We have land lines in our meeting rooms but not at workstations.

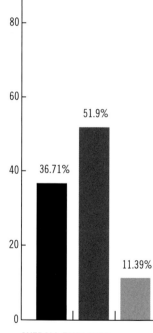

**OVERALL EMPLOYEE
IMPRESSION OF FORNEBU**

More Positive

As Expected

Less Positive

Not at all? Practically not at all. Which means that nearly everyone has only one number, and you will not find me, for example, labeled with any number in a directory in Norway with anything else than my mobile number.

If I get a call that enters into my voice mail, I can retrieve that voice mail from my portable PC. This enables me to carry forward a voice mail message to my neighbor, if I so want, if it is of relevance for others to know of a discussion that has been taking place on the voice mail platform.

And over time this becomes a new way of working, a new way of communicating efficiently with each other.

And how did you need to have the building support that new way of working with each other? The building is physically established with 220 security zones. We could basically have 220 competitors being looked after in this building without interfering with each other. But we are also able to allocate access between groups in our company in such a way that people can visit each other in a very easy manner. And we also created an environment—an atrium type of common area—where people could sit down, meet informally, and also be networked because it's a wireless access platform here as well. You will find groups of people, three to four persons, sitting in the atriums of this building in such a way that they have both a very nice, stimulating area to be in, as well as having the efficiency in place for that kind of communication.

Another key concept for the building was that there would be far fewer desks than there were people, because of the way this mobile technology liberates employees from their desks. In the 1990s, there were some famous failed experiments in this kind of corporate hot desking, like Chiat/Day in Los Angeles. What convinced you that it would work for Telenor in your new headquarters? I think this is an aspect which is very different from organization to organization. We have activity areas in Telenor that run one-to-one, desks and people, but then we have other environments that run one-to-one-point-five, which means that we are able, in particular in the marketing areas of our groups, to have more people than desks. This, of course, creates a new flexibility in how you operate your workforce.

WE CAN MOVE A THOUSAND PEOPLE FROM ONE SECTION TO ANOTHER SECTION OVER THE WEEKEND.

You know that any big company has a core structure for people-moving. You order the carpenters, you order all the handicraft men to adjust the new areas, and then come the computer guys afterwards to do the adjustments. Whereas in this building, we don't have that kind of obstacle. We can move a thousand people from one section to another section over the weekend, because there is no reprogramming; the portable PC is active and has the same profile wherever you are in the building. The moving cost, under a reorganization effort, for example, is close to zero.

As superbly functional as it is now, I imagine this way of working could have been a rather frightening idea for some staff when you were in the planning stages. How did you deal with that? Well, it was. It was scary for the corporate management as well as for the employees. So we developed a three-dimensional virtual-reality computer model to let people come and visit the new working area long before the buildings were really there. It also enabled us to, in a very lively way, execute the final setting of what these offices were to look like, including the colors and the views into the Norwegian scenery, because we also integrated daylight and sunlight into the 3D rooms, so we could get well associated with it in advance.

Then, corporate management—with myself as the main motivation force— ran a program where we really stimulated and motivated the middle management to take this environment into their own hands and make their own working habits, coming out of the cell-like type of offices into the more open space areas that we have here. These are not big spaces. I think the maximum number of workstations we have in one open space area is between 30 and 40.

At the same time there are some big spaces in the building. This is a very large building, is it not? It is a large building. Initially [before the move] we had 250,000 square meters and we took that down to 137,000, so we achieved quite a significant reduction in number of square meters. But this building is itself divided by eight entrances, and each is given a label—A, B, C, D. If I'm going to section number 7B I know that it's entrance B, seventh floor, so it's a very simple and unified structure to identify where I am in the building.

CHANGE TOOL IN ACTION: 15
MODEL IT / IMMERSIVE 4D MODEL

We built a virtual model of the building not to wow the audience but rather to show people how work can be different. Your office isn't a little place with a door on it anymore, it's the entire building. Throughout the day you will be in meetings in private conference rooms, in open spaces. You'll be in big lecture halls. You'll be at a desk, whichever one is available. You'll be on your cell phone walking through the plaza. That's the workplace.

We put the virtual model in a surround-screen, three-projector, immersive theater that held 25 people at a time. At least five days a week Telenor put staff through. The result was when people first arrived in the new building they knew what to do, they were happy, and it worked. I've seen much, much less change take place with disastrous results because nobody really knew what the change meant.

DUNCAN GRIFFIN
Senior Associate, NBBJ

Many people think the "future office" is an investment in technology, but it's not. It's an investment in people.

PETER PRAN
Principal, NBBJ

Once staff had actually moved in, how did they respond to this new environment, both in terms of locating themselves physically and also locating themselves as members of this company, this community? Here we really did so much preparatory work that the first group of employees who moved in here generated envy among those who hadn't moved in. Which means that when the next flow came, three months later, it all went smoothly.

You've done some surveys on how the staff feel about the new building. What did those show? We've run, on an annual basis, statistics on these kinds of questions. We have always received a high rating on how satisfied people feel about being here, and we have between four and five percent expressing a dissatisfaction with this kind of environment, which we probably would have anywhere.

So, the great majority are satisfied. They are satisfied, or they are even expressing that the environment here beats expectations. And this also has something to do with the exterior and where this building is placed, because it's located in one of the most magnificent areas, close to the Oslo fjord. So, from a scenic point of view it is a very beautiful site.

And the building is able to take advantage of that? The building plays on that. The building has been created in such a way, both by the selection of materials as well as from how windows are designed, to take advantage of the northern lighting, as well as the sunsets.

You've been in the building for several years now. How does it seem to be maturing, and how do you feel that Telenor is maturing with it? Well, we have to refresh ourselves on the original concept. We are also trying to get rid of some habits that we see and don't like. And as a CEO I urge all the working groups of this building to constantly debate and discuss the quality of work and how the environment functions.

And we see an interesting effect here: when we are hiring people from external sources they are fascinated by this type of environment, and we can really use the building and the structure as a differentiating factor. But also, as newcomers, they have not lived through the process of maturing into a regular way of operating, and some of these people are asking, "Where can I get an office? Where can I lock myself in?" And then we have to repeat the basic philosophy of the whole system.

When you first planned the building, what were you hoping it would communicate to people both inside and outside the company about Telenor? And how do you feel it is functioning in that regard? We feel that when we have visitors here who have something to do with Telenor in one way or another, they express fascination and they also express that, "Wow, I didn't expect something like this." The person who expressed this most clearly was Hewlett-Packard's [former CEO] Carly Fiorina, who was here for the opening in September 2002. She hadn't expected to see such a powerful building expressing as much as it did to her on first impact, which was for us an interesting reaction to note. We've seen it with several others who have come here.

You have many visitors, do you not? Remember that the general public can walk the plaza. This is an open area, even though it's an industrial area, and on a day like this I can look out the window and see people enjoying the sunset on the beach of the Oslo fjord. We have created an after-hours environment that is attractive, both for employees as well as for people living in the neighborhood. And on a yearly basis, 5,000 visitors tour the building.

So your experiment here is proving to be one that has applications elsewhere. We hope so. And we also find that a lot of Telenor customers come here and find inspiration for how to rearrange their own working environment using the combination of architecture, technology, and surroundings.

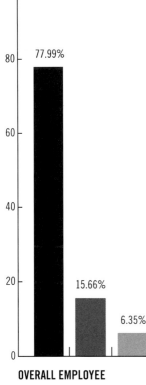

OVERALL EMPLOYEE
SATISFACTION AFTER TWO
MONTHS AT FORNEBU

■ More Positive

■ Unchanged

■ Less Positive

POWERS OF TEN

Telenor said that, although they have 7,500 employees, their ultimate teams are groups of 40. But they also know that collaboration happens in groups of four. And you've got to think about the one individual person. So we said, "Okay. Let's talk about an architecture that embraces 40 people and their coffee bar, their community space, their bulletin board." Every group of 40 has its own place, and within it, places for one and four. There are 10 groups of 40 around an atrium with a barista or a pool table.

So the next order of magnitude is 400. But you can still visualize your context: I'm in Building Number Seven, and in it are a bunch of groups of 40. Each of those buildings of 400 latches onto embracing arms that are huge circulation paths and atriums. And those arms embrace the open gathering place in the plaza. So, walking into the building you go from being one to four to 40 to 400 to 4,000. The scale of the architecture matches the increases, so you never feel lost.

SCOTT WYATT
Partner, NBBJ

Telenor customers come here and find inspiration for how to rearrange their own working environment using architecture, technology, and surroundings.

PETER PRAN
Principal, NBBJ

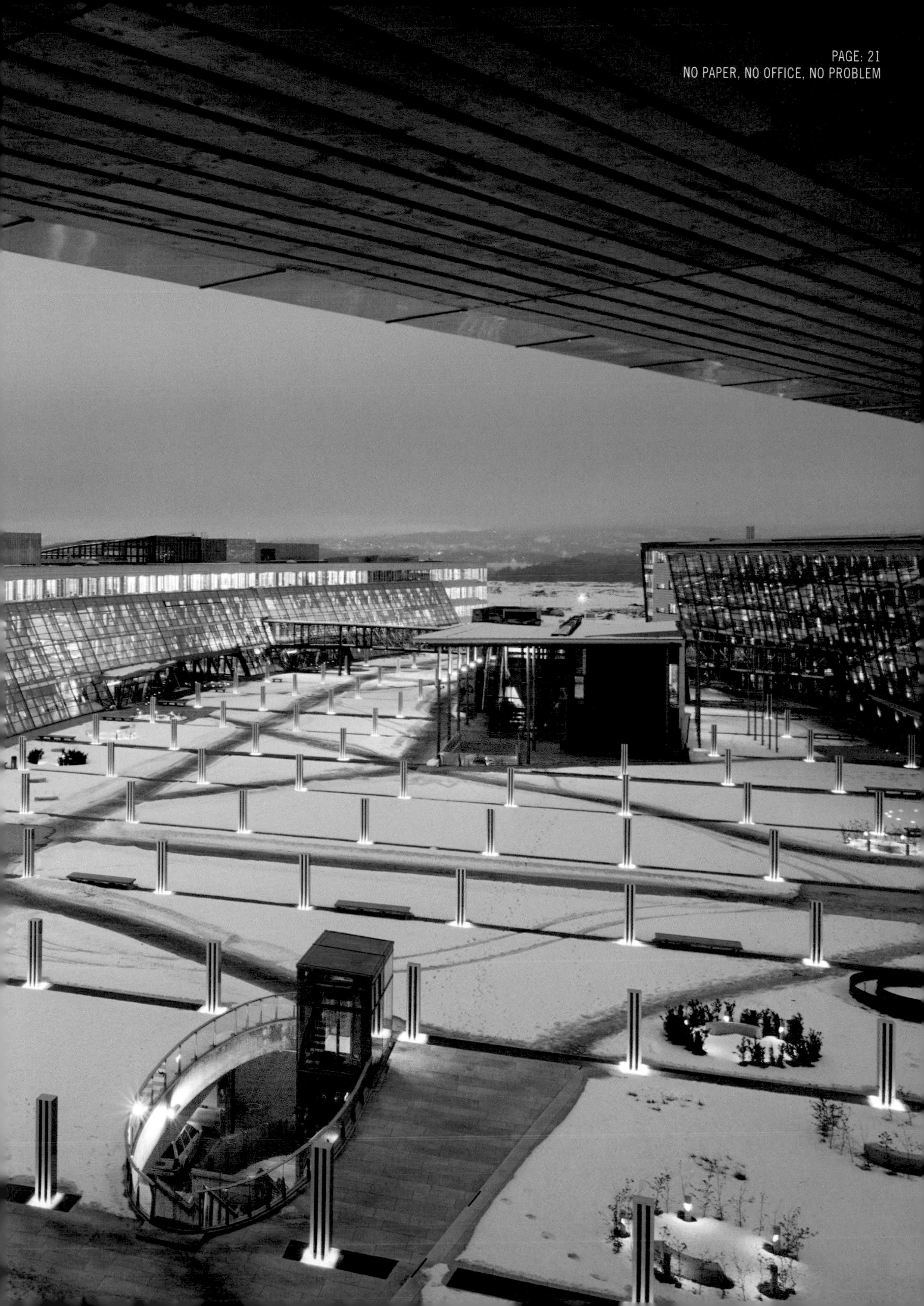

As you continue to develop new products and services, how will the building and its infrastructure accommodate them? There are constant changes in how our communication platform is delivering new functionality to its users, and we are developing those kinds of functionality enhancements at top speed.

And the building is able to accommodate those shifts? Absolutely. We have not yet encountered an obstacle in that sense. We have already upgraded the wireless access platform for PCs, because the wireless technology has developed tremendously over the last four years.

And that has been something that you've been able to accomplish without a lot of trouble and money? Of course, any migration is not free, but being a technology company, this is our profession, so when we're doing something like this, based on our needs, we reckon that there are customers out there who will be interested in the same functionality enhancements. That's how this market moves, and we've been able to meet that kind of development.

As part of your growth as an international company you've been looking at markets in central and eastern Europe and in Asia. What future does the Fornebu model have in those cultures? That's an interesting question. In 2005 we inaugurated a new office building in Kiev, in the Ukraine; we will open a new office building in Malaysia; and we are in the midst of establishing a new office building in Islamabad in Pakistan. All these buildings are taking elements from Fornebu, but they are not going as far as we have on the standardization of the workstations, because these are societies which are more hierarchical than the Scandinavian societies. But from a technology point of view, with integration of mobile and PC services, we have more or less the same standards.

And we see that our local managers pick up the ideas here from our head office and use them back home when they make their decisions on how they want to sit, want to work, want to create working environments for the employees. ✦

LEARNING BY HEART

The Cleveland Clinic Heart Center, Cleveland, Completion 2008.

We've grown from 125 doctors when I arrived to 1,800 doctors now. We're at 95 percent occupancy and have trouble finding beds for patients. We have rooms that have been in use since 1928. So we need to update and expand.

DR. TOBY COSGROVE
CEO, The Cleveland Clinic Foundation

The problem with so many city hospitals is that they can't expand. Cleveland Clinic was trying to shoehorn bits and pieces into the existing campus. We said, "You need to be more radical."

FRIEDRICH K.M. BÖHM
Partner, NBBJ

Our institution is about innovation. When the organization's model came about 80 years ago it was viewed as Communism because it was so different. The people who inhabited the building and put it together were risk-takers.

T.C.

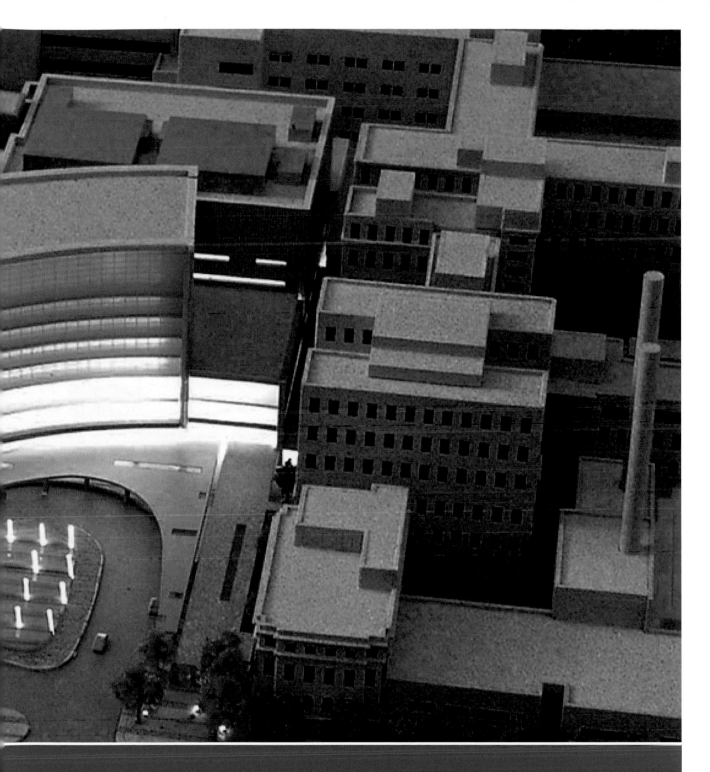

ost hospitals have professional management and there's conflict etween the caregivers and the people ho run the hospital. Cleveland Clinic is very successful business, but it is a inic—led and run by physicians.

3.

Being both the user and the administrator gives me a different perspective. I know that cardiac surgeons no longer have much in common with liver surgeons, but have lots in common with cardiac anesthesiologists. This new space gives me the opportunity to reorganize the clinic around organ systems—institutes

rather than departments. Say you have a headache. Do you go to a neurosurgeon, a neurologist, a psychiatrist? Go to the neurologic institute and they'll sort it out for you.

T.C.

They had a 1,500-car parking garage at the entrance to the clinic that blocked their ability to develop. We said, "Tear down the garage and build a new heart center right in front of everything."

F.B.

One of my goals was to beautify our area of Euclid Avenue, Cleveland's old main street. NBBJ spent six months listening to our people and came back with a design where the new heart center became the gateway for the Cleveland Clinic.

DR. FLOYD LOOP
Former CEO, The Cleveland Clinic Foundation

The entrance to a place makes a statement about the institution. As you walk into Grand Central Station you say, "Wow." There's going to be a wow factor here.

T.C.

hen you walk in the door you're going to el confident that you're in the right ace for your healthcare.

The new lobby will accommodate everybody who comes in and out of the clinic—up to 25,000 people a day. So what we are dealing with is the gateway to a small city.

F.B.

It's going to be a stunner of a building that allows us to attract both patients and doctors. And that's the combination that really makes medicine happen.

T.C.

HEALTHY BONES

How does one of America's largest health-care companies create a system to serve one of America's fastest growing regions? Banner Health did it by building Banner Estrella, a Phoenix hospital that mimics natural desert growth to create a model for modular expansion.

PHOENIX-BASED BANNER HEALTH IS ONE OF THE LARGEST, NON-PROFIT HEALTHCARE SYSTEMS IN THE COUNTRY, WITH 20 HOSPITALS IN SEVEN WESTERN STATES: ALASKA, ARIZONA, CALIFORNIA, COLORADO, NEBRASKA, NEVADA, AND WYOMING.

BANNER ESTRELLA IS THE FIRST GROUND-UP HOSPITAL TO COME ONLINE AS PART OF BANNER HEALTH'S DEVELOPMENT PROGRAM IN THIS REGION.

ACCORDING TO 2002 US CENSUS DATA, THE SOUTHWEST IS THE FASTEST-GROWING REGION IN THE UNITED STATES, AND THE SUBURBS OF PHOENIX ARE AMONG THE NATION'S FASTEST GROWING CITIES.

LOCATED ON 50 ACRES IN WEST PHOENIX, THE NEW HOSPITAL INCLUDES A FULL-SERVICE, 167-BED ACUTE CARE TOWER, MEDICAL OFFICE BUILDINGS, AND AN OUTPATIENT SURGERY CENTER.

THE MEDICAL CAMPUS PROVIDES SURGERY, CANCER CARE, CARDIAC SERVICES, EMERGENCY SERVICES, AND A COMPREHENSIVE WOMEN AND INFANTS PROGRAM. IT IS CURRENTLY ABLE TO HANDLE 4,000 BIRTHS PER YEAR.

THE HOSPITAL IS DESIGNED FOR SYSTEMATIC GROWTH: IT CAN ACCOMMODATE A 10- TO 20-YEAR GROWTH PLAN BY ADDING TWO ADDITIONAL TOWERS, FOR A TOTAL OF 600 BEDS. ALL NON-BIRTHING PATIENT ROOMS ARE UNIVERSALLY-SIZED AND ADAPTABLE TO DIFFERENT LEVELS OF CARE.

IT IS A "PAPER-LIGHT" FACILITY, INCORPORATING COMPUTERIZED PATIENT DOCUMENTATION AND A PHYSICIAN ORDER ENTRY SYSTEM.

INFORMATION TECHNOLOGY HAS ELIMINATED THE TRADITIONAL NURSE STATION. INSTEAD OF A CENTRAL NURSE HUB, THE HOSPITAL'S CLINICAL INTEGRATION SUITE INCLUDES ALL THE ACUTE CARE AND CRITICAL CARE NURSING FUNCTIONS.

A NEW CAREGIVING MODEL BREAKS DOWN THE TRADITIONAL CLINICAL SILOS. HERE, SURGERY, CARDIAC, AND IMAGING SERVICES SHARE A SINGLE CLEAN CORE.

SUSAN S. DORIA
SENIOR VICE PRESIDENT, STRATEGIC DEVELOPMENT, BANNER HEALTH

Susan Doria was named Senior Vice President of Strategic Development for Banner Health in October 2002. She is responsible for business and organizational development across Banner Health, which was formed in 1999 through the merger of Samaritan Health System and Lutheran Health Systems. Doria oversees the company-wide functions of Planning, Development and Construction, Learning and Communications, Brand Services, and Grants and Appropriations. Prior to this role, Doria, who joined Samaritan Health System in 1986, served in a series of staff and executive positions. She received both a Bachelor of Science degree and Master of Health Services Administration degree from Arizona State University. Doria devotes many hours of community work as the Board Chair of HomeBase Youth Services, a non-profit agency helping homeless youth.

Phoenix, Arizona, is one of the fastest-growing cities in the United States. Can you tell me where that population boom is coming from and why it's happening? Phoenix has become the fifth-largest metropolitan area in the country. It has an attractive climate and a growing cultural, retail, and education base. It also has reasonable housing costs and significant growth in new jobs. Most of our migration comes from California, and the Midwest is a close second behind that. In the past decade, it has really boomed and there doesn't seem to be an end in sight. We're reaching a critical mass now where there're interesting architecture and sophisticated activities for people who are quite cosmopolitan.

What did your research tell you about the healthcare needs of this incoming population? We've been looking to make a major investment in growth to keep up with the population boom and we've started to think about the types of facilities we would design to accommodate this growth. First and foremost, it's about picking the right location, and second it's about adaptable design. We're having a hard time retrofitting and renovating many of our existing facilities to adapt to the changes in care delivery that we're seeing today and will continue to see into the future. We had to think about it relative to new technologies and how spaces and places would have to change to adapt to the technology. One thing we've found in all of our healthcare planning to date, going back a couple decades, is that there wasn't enough forethought in terms of how to make space much more flexible as technology changes.

Before you started to build Banner Estrella in west Phoenix, what healthcare facilities did Banner have in the Phoenix area? We have eight hospitals in Arizona, seven in the metropolitan Phoenix area. We were already the major healthcare player in town, with upwards of a third of the market share. We saw an opportunity to go into an underserved area that had not been addressed from a hospital need perspective because hospitals' operating performance had been depressed for a while. Many of our competitors didn't have the financial wherewithal to invest in new facilities. When we had the ability to invest, we jumped on the opportunity to go into that new community and build a new campus for it.

CHANGE TOOL IN ACTION: 02
LET VISION DRIVE THE PROGRAMMING

We invited visionaries and leaders from healthcare institutions across the nation and asked them to speak to us about the future of healthcare: What should the hospital of the future be? What kind of services would be provided and what kind of issues are going to be important? What role does technology play in this and how do the humanitarian issues play into this kind of delivery? This exercise got us beyond the tyranny of designing and programming for first use — for the present only.

JOHN PANGRAZIO
Partner, NBBJ

As part of the visioning sessions, we invited about 150 people, mostly Banner employees or representatives from the community. We broke down into groups and each group included an architect from the design team. The groups spent two to three hours building a model from a kit of parts of what they felt the vision of the hospital for the future should be.

JOHN PANGRAZIO
Partner, NBBJ

Some teams tried to build as best they could and some did more abstract solutions that mirrored what they felt were the key issues. All the groups came to the conclusion that the hospital for the future is very different than what they had been building or what they had at present.

At the end, they said, "We need to develop Banner as a system; we need to develop a prototype of a hospital that becomes a platform, if not a chassis, to beta test various issues and innovations."

SCOTT DUNLAP
Senior Associate, NBBJ

Banner Estrella was built, for a hospital, extraordinarily fast—36 months from the time the design team started to the time the hospital actually opened. Why such an accelerated schedule? Being one of the first to market is important for our industry. We had new competitors coming into the area—there was one hospital that opened about a year before we did, so we didn't want to have too much lag time here. There was also a lot of demand for the Banner product from area community leaders and interest from physicians who wanted to expand their practices and preferred to do it with Banner.

What implications did a fast-track schedule like that have initially for the design? Getting clarity of the overall concept on the front end was a key driver. We thought of this as our franchise model for future campuses, because we knew that other market segments were also growing quickly. When we started design work we saw this as the launch of Banner's "Hospital for the Future." We weren't just designing the hospital that sits on this site, we were designing Banner's model for tomorrow's hospital. We had inclusive, multidisciplinary stakeholder involvement on the front end to explore what we needed to take into consideration. And frankly, because of all the problems we have with our current facilities, this concept became almost like marching orders for the design group. Address these problems and do not design like today's environment. Think about how care is changing, think about how clinicians and teams of people are interacting, think about what's important in the healing process. Get beyond any biases you have about healthcare and how it should be delivered today. Start with fresh eyes, from the patient perspective.

What are some of the problems that you're having today in the facilities that you're trying to retrofit? One of the biggest problems we face is that campuses weren't designed to accommodate growth over time, yet they always have to grow and add more beds as the population fills in. Unfortunately, your core chassis isn't flexible; you have hard-wall departments next to each other and there is no room to expand. So the facility doesn't flex for growth; it also doesn't flex for changes in technology, equipment that's getting smaller or equipment that's getting much larger. So it's really hard, if you didn't design the campus to flex with growth demands, to go back and retrofit it later.

*Can you describe how the growth design that is built right into the new facility
works?* The concept is pretty simple. The building is organized along a central
spine with all the special mechanical, electrical, and plumbing needed to create
patient-safe spaces. If you don't plan from that kind of guts, it becomes very
expensive to move these systems later on. The diagnostic and treatment components, which change over time as new modalities of care arise, are designed to
be much more like medical office space. They're designed like a honeycomb. You
start on a grid pattern with the smallest D&T area that you need, and then you
build on that grid pattern as your growth goes. Patient care towers are also modular. Each tower can hold almost 200 beds. We can add towers, without disrupting
the first one or any of the central spine.

Has this become the model that you were referring to earlier? Yes. It's a brilliant
design in the way that you can grow something over time without disrupting
current operations. And that's the problem: how do you ever close down a hospital to do a major construction project? From a patient care perspective, where
would those patients go? And think of all the revenue you'd lose during that year
of construction.

And this allows you to respond to the market need. Right, exactly.

So the term that you referred to earlier, "Hospital for the Future," for Banner literally meant what? We had eight components that made our Hospital for the Future. One of the first is flexible and adaptable design; that's the whole piece that I've been talking about. Another major component involves creating a healing environment. There's been a lot of research done about music, light, color, texture, smell, how you use space and bring the outdoors in and so forth, that has really impacted the design of healthcare facilities so it can contribute to better patient care outcomes.

How do those theories actually get incorporated into the building itself?
Lighting, just as an example, is very important, so the patient rooms are designed with access to windows and lots of sunlight. Another component is patient-centered care. The rooms are designed to accommodate family members who spend the night, because the family is now involved in the caregiving process and has become much more like a patient advocate. You have to be very clever about how you design different zones of care—including sterile environments for the clinician—so that there's maximum efficiency of the space, and a lot more efficiency of staff time, too. We were also looking at how to improve patient care outcomes, so we have designed what are called acuity-adaptable rooms. In many hospitals, patients start off in the ICU after very intensive surgery, go to a step-down unit and then to a regular medical surgical bed before they go home. In the course of those hand-offs they're with different caregivers and may be on different floors. Orders, directions, care become fragmented. There's room for human error. In the acuity adaptable model, we have a core of rooms on each floor that go up and down in intensity of care and the patient doesn't have to move anywhere.

Another aspect of the "Hospital for the Future" is something called "paper light," which is not quite the same as paperless, but is heading in that direction.
Estrella is the first place that Banner has installed a completely electronic environment, where nearly all documentation is done electronically. We have stations both in and outside of the room where clinicians can pull up records and make notes electronically. We watched videos of what usually happens on nursing floors and saw how much time the nurse or physician spends walking around looking

for the patient chart. It adds to time delays and information isn't always collected appropriately in the patient chart. Making this electronic is not only very efficient, it also improves quality of care, because you can build in systems that actually have rules to check things that have been ordered. With everything electronic, there are many new tools that can enhance the clinician's ability to deliver better quality care.

How much have these tools been applied, to your knowledge, in other hospital settings? Not a whole lot yet. It's a very expensive investment, and there's a lot of push-back from people in the system because it changes the way things are done. You have to invest time in redesigning your care processes. So, we were really excited to have the opportunity to install this from top to bottom in a whole new facility, where both the staff and the doctors who were recruited to the facility knew that this was the expectation.

And the care and the efficiency benefits—are they showing up demonstrably yet? We've been open about seven months, so it is too early to measure. Now, from a care satisfaction perspective we're hitting the mark. We do patient satisfaction surveys and benchmark ourselves. They're done by a third party and we're measured against other peer organizations around the country. Estrella's hitting the 99th percentile in patient satisfaction. For the rest of Banner's hospitals, in aggregate, we're trying to get to the top quartile, which is the 75th percentile. As a system, some of our hospitals are in the 40th percentile and we're trying to move them up to the 75th. Estrella's already hitting the top, because the facility is wonderful, the care experience is wonderful, people have new tools to provide better care.

There's another kind of amenity that Estrella offers, which is a bit harder to quantify: the building itself is designed to be a meditative, contemplative place. How did that concept evolve? When we thought about healthcare for the future, we didn't think of it just as an episodic, single event that impacts just one part of the body. We thought about the fact that it is an experience, and that experiences really do transform people. Then we said, "How can the space allow someone an opportunity to go more inside themselves, peacefully, to think about what the impact of

CHANGE TOOL IN ACTION: 07
CREATE CHAMPIONS FOR THE VISION
Banner Estrella's vision was about reorganizing the hospital delivery organization to shift it to a more collaborative culture, reduce redundancy, share resources, and improve patient safety. This would require a level of behavioral change beyond what designers and administrators could mandate. It meant a change in the cultural currency of the traditional healthcare organization.

MACKENZIE SKENE
Partner, NBBJ

Banner's leadership enlisted key physicians and administrators, people who believed in the potential of reorganization. They became the enablers of a new practice vision. These were people who didn't wait for a "green light." They stepped right up to address naysayers. They provided clarification and responded to objections. They propelled the ideas about the merits of the model through all levels of the organization. It was these people who breathed life into the vision, gave it legs and purpose. Without their talents and purposefulness, Banner Estrella would have never been realized.

CHARLES MARTIN
Principal, NBBJ

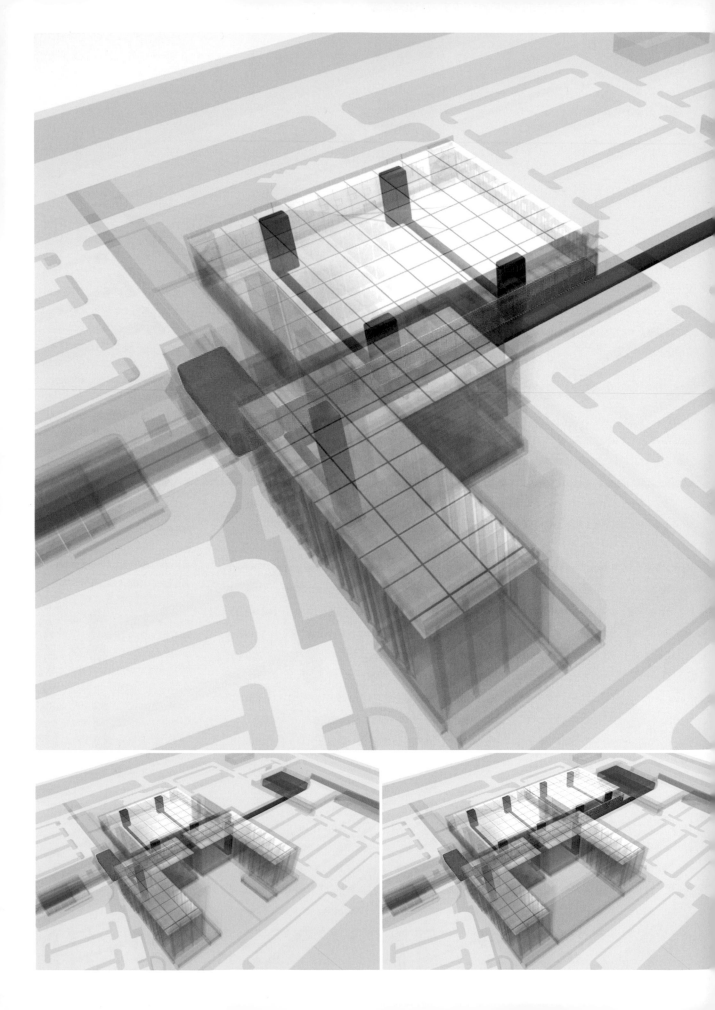

HOSPITAL FOR THE FUTURE

Few industries encounter as much continuous change as the healthcare industry. And yet, the facilities in which they are housed have typically been optimized for their first use, rather than for the inevitable subsequent uses that they will encounter. On almost any healthcare campus, you see a collection of building additions, each built for a specific use, unable to adapt. Banner embraced the hospital for the future as a key organizing concept for Estrella and for future campuses. The hospital for the future is designed to adapt to unknown futures—shifts to outpatient care, increasing acuity of inpatient care, and emerging diagnostic and treatment technologies.

As the frequency of change continues to increase, each change cycle is a fraction of a building's life. We are aware that some things, such as human need for clarity, the distribution of energy, have a greater sense of permanence—slower cycles of change. Things like care delivery methods and medical technology are more temporal — rapid cycles of change.

Healthcare design must facilitate change and growth, contribute to healing, be affordable in first cost, and remain effective in the long term. Given this perspective, we've developed a framework for design, "auto-genesis," that enables a facility to "self-create." It organizes the building into permanent zones for integrated circulation and infrastructure, and temporal zones for rapid change with minimized disruption and cost. By keeping permanent infrastructure out of the spaces that allow for change, the redevelopment of these areas is significantly less costly and disruptive.

The simple analogy is to a city; the permanent areas are the streets used for circulation, containing all of the utilities. This establishes a rational system for growth. The spaces between the streets, the city blocks, are available for development and redevelopment over time.

At Estrella, an open-ended infrastructure and materials flow "spine" becomes a major organizing element to which adaptable, universal space fields attach. The open-ended nature of the spine enables expansion without disruption. The spaces fields, unencumbered by major infrastructure penetrations, are set up for rapid change as the healthcare needs of this community change over time.

RICHARD DALLAM
Partner, NBBJ

IT'S A BRILLIANT DESIGN IN THE WAY THAT YOU CAN GROW SOMETHING OVER TIME WITHOUT DISRUPTING CURRENT OPERATIONS.

that transformation is." So, a lot of control is built into the mechanics of the patient care experience so that you aren't feeling like things are being done to you. You're the leader in this experience and you can go as deep as you want into your own transformation or not. The space is designed to be quiet and reflective.

What kind of feedback have you been getting from staff since the opening?
We're very lucky because we planned well, I would say, to select people who were going to feel comfortable in this kind of an environment and who were going to help us successfully take the physical structure into reality. Because it's one thing to design a building and then it's another to operate it the way that you envisioned. And so we had a selection and hiring process and an on-boarding process through orientation that was very deliberate, very specific. We actually had people audition for their jobs; we had them role play. At a new facility you often will get five applicants for every one new opening and, because of this, we had the ability to be very selective about the people we hired. We were very clear about the kind of environment we were hoping to create, what the design of the facility was supposed to contribute to, and what the role of the associate—we don't even call them employees—was at Estrella. It's one thing to create a new stage, but if you're doing the same old play you've missed the whole opportunity. I think we've done a good job. A start-up is always challenging, and we've had some adjustments along the way, but we did a lot of work on what the associate experience was going to be like and how it was going to be different than any other employee experience in any of our other hospitals. For the most part, I think folks have been feeling that the experience that we described to them, that we hoped they would help us deliver for the patient, is also working for them.

It's extraordinary that all that was accomplished in 36 months. You designed the future! If you start out with the future in mind, and get everybody there first, the to-dos are pretty easy. Nobody's fighting. You always go back to your touchstone: "We're a hospital for the future." That was our guiding star. "Estrella" means star in Spanish. With that guiding star to go back to, it was easy to make decisions about which way to go, because the vision was really clear.

100 —

99th

84th

80 —

60 —

40 —

20 —

0 —

PRESS GANEY PATIENT SATISFACTION SCORES FOR INPATIENT HOSPITALS

 National Average

Banner Estrella

* Source: 2004 National Inpatient Priority Index, Press Ganey. Reflects average mean score; survey of over 2 million patients treated at over 1,500 U.S. hospitals.

DESERT MEDITATION

The design team was coming from the Pacific Northwest. If you go into the forest you can find five, seven, eight layers of life from the forest floor to the canopy—it's life crowding in upon life. What better source of inspiration for the team than the desert they found themselves in because the desert is singular in a very different way. There, you might find a plant with a 10-foot radius around it before you find the next plant. The desert is strong and it's severe but it also focuses the attention; there was so much there to learn about making a meditative space.

The design concept started with observations about the desert floor—it's vast, flat, weathered land that's punctuated positively by things like mesas and negatively by things like canyons. And as soon as there's an event in the landscape, either positive or negative or both, life forms— especially in the cuts, like canyons, which are where you find water. When you add the desert sun to those events, the landscape becomes a huge clock, clearly expressing the passage of time.

The building was conceived of as one of those desert intersections of something additive, which is the building coming up out of the ground, with something subtractive, which is the exterior garden space enclosed between significant parts of the building. It was conceived of as a place of contemplation. A place to focus on the significant events that occur throughout one's life.

CHRISTIAN CARLSON
Principal, NBBJ

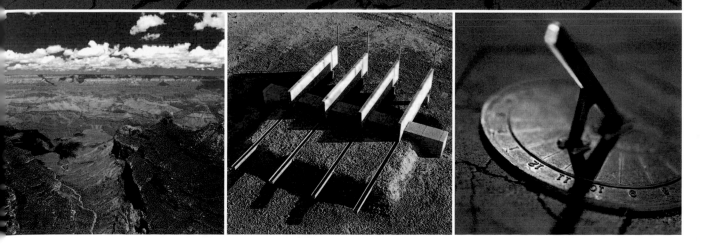

Hospital buildings easily last 50 to 75 years. Imagine how much healthcare has changed over that time and how much it's going to change.

CHARLES MARTIN
Principal, NBBJ

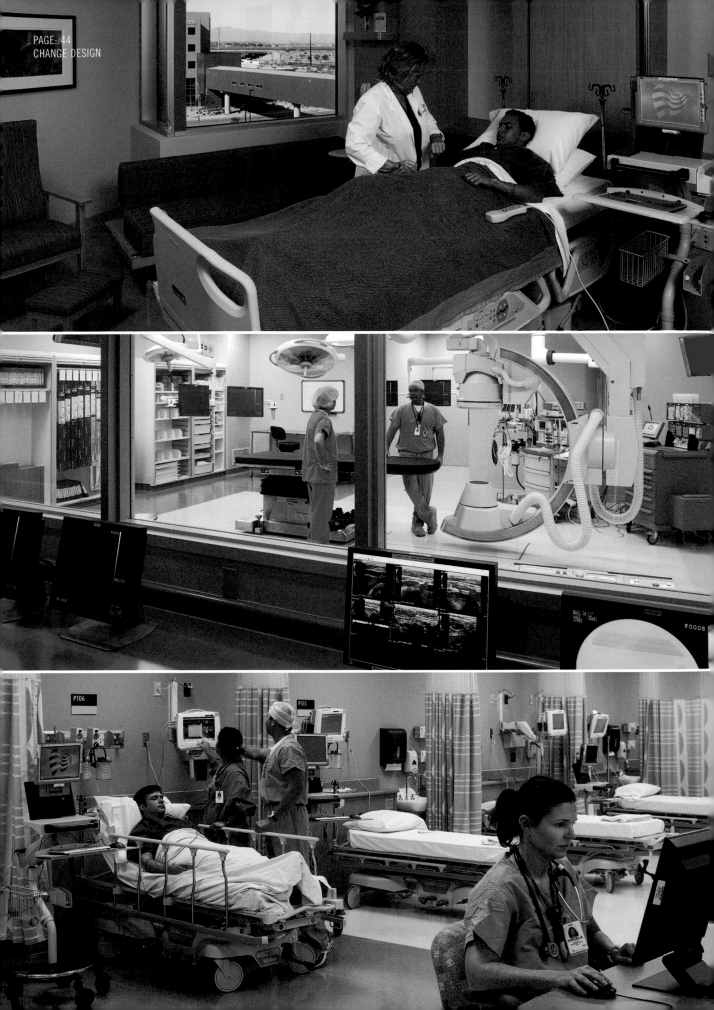

WE'RE A HOSPITAL FOR THE FUTURE. THAT WAS OUR GUIDING STAR. "ESTRELLA" MEANS STAR IN SPANISH. WITH THAT TO GO BACK TO, IT WAS EASY TO MAKE DECISIONS.

Since you created Estrella as a franchise model, are there things that you'll be changing in the next facility, having had the experience of building the first one?
It's important to make sure that the facility reflects the market that you're going into and the demographic you'll be serving. That impacts where it's located, how it all fits into that environment, and the mix of services that you'll provide. We have been able to take the essence of the design and site-adapt it. For example, Estrella is a high-tech facility and more contemplative because of the intensity of care while the next facility we're doing, Banner Gateway, is more of a general community hospital. It won't, for example, have open-heart surgery capability or high-intensity cardiac services there; it's going to have more obstetrics and pediatrics. So it will have a less contemplative feel and more of a sense of community. There will be more of a sense of energy and vitality. And yet the overall concept of a flexible, adaptable healing environment, centered around the patient, will still be there. It will just morph slightly to accommodate the different activity going on. We're on a 30-month schedule for Gateway, so we've shaved off six months because we started with this franchise model. Now we're taking it out to our third project, which is actually going to start not as a hospital but as an ambulatory outpatient center and will grow into a hospital. So design, in terms of how you design to accommodate all that, has been very important. ✦

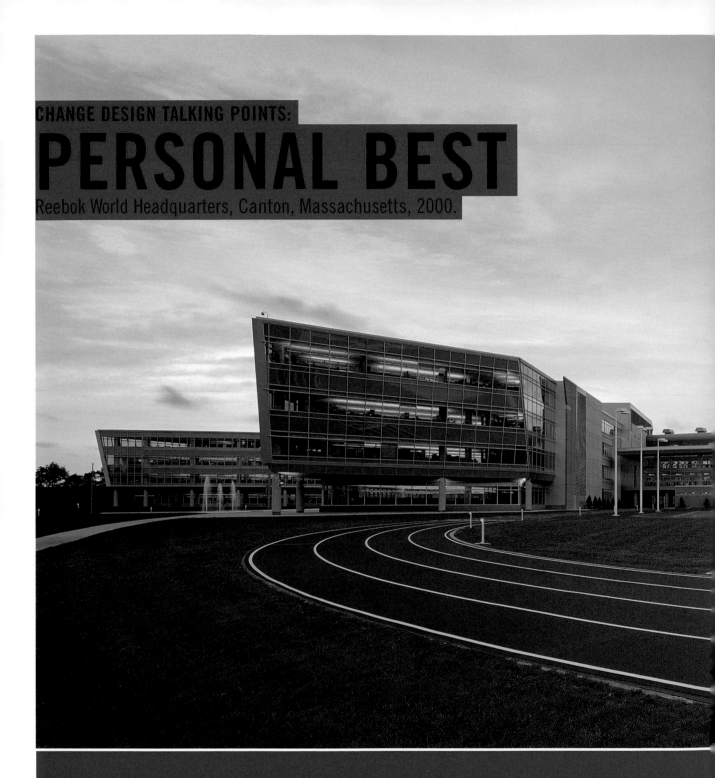

CHANGE DESIGN TALKING POINTS:
PERSONAL BEST

Reebok World Headquarters, Canton, Massachusetts, 2000.

Reebok asked us to answer the question, "What is Reebok? We're involved in all these different activities — golf, football, the Olympics, fitness — and we want this headquarters to inspire our enterprise."

STEVE McCONNELL
Partner, NBBJ

I said, "I don't want an office park. I want a place that is the spirit of innovation!"

PAUL FIREMAN
Founder and former CEO, Reebok

Our answer was simple — the Reebok spirit is the collective energy of their sports and fitness activities. So we set out to create a headquarters that marries the workforce to that energy and leaves no doubt as to the aspiration of the enterprise.

S.M.

e idea was to tell the story of Reebok
hout articulating it in words.

Sports equipment implies movement. So
we allowed the movement of sports to,
quite literally, describe and "inscribe"
the design of the building, inside and out.

JONATHAN WARD
Principal, NBBJ

What surrounds the building is what it
stands for — playing fields and courts.

P.E.

The fitness center is integrated into the building, so you can hear the squeak of a basketball shoe in the lobby. That sound provides clarity—it reflects a place where employees and their work converge and energize each other.

ALAN YOUNG
Principal, NBBJ

It's a new type of workplace that integrates all aspects of the client's business. It brings together the employees and their culture of athleticism with Reebok's products and their intended uses.

S.M.

There was a commitment to the concep from everyone on the team. Everyone owned a bit of the design. Everyone made a valuable contribution. There w no template—just ideas and dialogue

DOUG NOONAN
Director, Corporate Real Estate and Facilities, Reebok

e place feels alive — and that's had an pact on our product innovation. Since oving in, we've realized a double-digit crease in the value of our stock.

When you come into the building you know what you are and who you are. We are a sports brand, and this is our church. Everything that comes out of our church — products, innovation, marketing — represents who we are.

PAUL BROWN
Vice President, Product Design, Reebok

The new headquarters has changed the way our people think of the business when they wake up in the morning. They're living the brand experience. I view this as a renaissance, a complete regrouping.

P.F.

IN PLANE VIEW

Boeing Vice President Carolyn Corvi transformed an earthquake into a window of opportunity, building a factory-office hybrid where engineers, mechanics, support personnel and the program leadership share a workplace and a common outlook.

ONE OF FOUR OPERATING GROUPS WITHIN THE BOEING COMPANY, COMMERCIAL AIRPLANES IS HEADQUARTERED IN RENTON, WASHINGTON. IT IS ORGANIZED INTO THREE PRIMARY BUSINESS UNITS— AIRPLANE PROGRAM, THE 787 DREAMLINER PROGRAM, AND COMMERCIAL AVIATION SERVICES—OPERATING OUT OF RENTON AND EVERETT, WASHINGTON, AND LONG BEACH, CALIFORNIA.

THE BOEING 737 IS THE MOST WIDELY USED COMMERCIAL JETLINER IN HISTORY, ACCOUNTING FOR NEARLY ONE-THIRD OF ALL COMMERCIAL JETLINERS IN SERVICE. EACH DAY, THE MORE THAN 4,000 737S THAT ARE IN SERVICE WORLDWIDE CARRY A COMBINED TOTAL OF ABOUT 1.3 MILLION PASSENGERS. EVERY 4.6 SECONDS, A 737 TAKES OFF OR LANDS SOMEWHERE ON THE GLOBE.

BOEING'S 278-ACRE RENTON SITE ENCOMPASSES 4.1 MILLION SQUARE FEET (380,902 SQUARE METERS) OF BUILDING SPACE. THROUGHOUT THE YEARS, RENTON HAS BEEN HOME TO MANY OF COMMERCIAL AVIATION'S BEST KNOWN AIRPLANES, INCLUDING THE 707, 727, AND THE ORIGINAL MODELS OF THE 737 AND 757. TODAY, EMPLOYEES THERE PRODUCE THE POPULAR BOEING NEXT GENERATION 737.

THE GROUND FLOOR OF THE FINAL ASSEMBLY BUILDING FOR THE BOEING 737 COVERS 760,000 SQUARE FEET (70,600 SQUARE METERS)—APPROXIMATELY TWO CITY BLOCKS. ACTIVITIES AT OTHER MAIN BUILDINGS AT THE RENTON SITE INCLUDE WING-LINE PRODUCTION AND A PAINT HANGAR.

BOEING BECAME THE FIRST COMMERCIAL AIRFRAME MANUFACTURER TO USE A MOVING ASSEMBLY LINE TO BUILD JETLINERS WHEN THE PRODUCTION LINES WERE TRANSFORMED FROM SEMI-STATIONARY PRODUCTION LINES TO A CONTINUOUSLY MOVING LINE. THE AIRPLANES ON THE LINE MOVE CONTINUOUSLY AT A RATE OF TWO INCHES (FIVE CENTIMETERS) PER MINUTE; THE LINE STOPS ONLY FOR EMPLOYEE BREAKS, CRITICAL PRODUCTION ISSUES, OR SHIFT CHANGES.

THE MOVING LINE WAS ONE OF SEVERAL TECHNIQUES INTRODUCED AS PART OF THE ADOPTION OF "LEAN MANUFACTURING" PRINCIPLES. LEAN PRACTICE INVOLVES CHANGING A WORK AREA OR A BUSINESS PROCESS TO MAXIMIZE EFFICIENCY, IMPROVE QUALITY AND SAFETY, ELIMINATE UNNECESSARY MOTION AND INVENTORY, AND SAVE TIME. COMMERCIAL AIRPLANES BEGAN IMPLEMENTING LEAN PRACTICES IN 1993.

CAROLYN CORVI
VICE PRESIDENT – GENERAL MANAGER, AIRPLANE PRODUCTION, BOEING COMMERCIAL AIRPLANES

Carolyn Corvi is Vice President – General Manager of Airplane Production. She is responsible for managing Boeing Commercial Airplanes' fully integrated production system from design through production and delivery. Created in 2005, the Airplane Production organization combines the former Supplier Management organization with all commercial airplane production activities in Everett, Auburn, and Renton, Washington, and Long Beach, California.

Prior to this assignment Corvi was Vice President and General Manager of the 737/757 programs. Under her leadership, the 737/757 programs incorporated industry-leading applications of lean manufacturing principles. Corvi joined Boeing in 1974 and has held a variety of key leadership assignments. For her contributions to both the company and aerospace industry, Corvi won the 2001 Women in Aerospace Leadership award. She currently serves on Virginia Mason Medical Center's Health System Board of Directors and is on the president's advisory board at Embry-Riddle Aeronautical University.

Let's start by talking about the Boeing 737. When this project began you were the vice president in charge of the Boeing 737 programs. What is the history of that plane in the marketplace? The 737 has a long history at Boeing that goes back to 1967. Completely redesigned 10 years ago, today's 737 is called the Next Generation 737 and it's part of the Boeing tradition of designing airplane families. The 737 family includes the 737-600, the 737-700, the 737-800 and the 737-900ER. In dual-class configuration, the 737-600 seats 110 people and the 737-900ER, for example, seats 180 but can seat up to 215 people in a single class. It's a very capable family of airplanes. It's the longest running and best-selling commercial jet in history with more than 6,000 sold and we continue to be very competitive in this size of airplane.

When you first started thinking about the idea of rebuilding the facility at Renton, what were the opportunities and challenges that the 737 program was facing? In 2001, as the year began, the market conditions were quite strong. We were selling into an up market and demand was high. But then a confluence of local and world events happened that had a major impact on business. We had an earthquake in the area in February 2001 which damaged several of our buildings. September 11th changed security in airports and, as we all know, had a significant impact on the airline industry. Later in 2003, the SARS epidemic in Asia, more terrorist attacks, and the war in Iraq were all detrimental to the industry.

So we went from a boom of the early part of 2001, when we started to think about how we could transform the work environment for our people, to the bust at the end of the year. That rapid business downturn and the uncertainty about when it would bounce back gave us even more reason to change. We were faced with an opportunity. We didn't relish the situation, because of all the external conditions forced on us, but it was the perfect time to do something different. We knew we could take advantage of the downtime in the marketplace.

At the time that all of these factors were coming together, the 737s were being assembled in the facility at Renton that Boeing had been using since the 1960s. What was the factory like? The Renton factory was a vast building with high bays, cement floors, exposed structural beams, and open mezzanine storage areas for parts and tools. We used overhead cranes to move parts of the airplanes and heavy equipment

CHANGE TOOL IN ACTION: 06
WORK WITH CHANGE AGENTS

Within every large organization is a mix of people with differing perspectives and opinions. Their perceived objectives within the organization can sometimes be seen as divergent. This is one reason change can be so difficult. Boeing's Commercial Airlines Division had a leader with a clear vision of what she was trying to accomplish with this project. This vision, its conceptualization, the drive to be more efficient by bringing the mechanics and engineers together, came from her division. The design team's job was to work with her and her division as the primary agents of change and other entities within Boeing to achieve a win-win solution for all stakeholders.

LORI WALKER
Principal, NBBJ

IF THERE'S A PROBLEM WITH A PRODUCT, IT'S NOT THE MECHANIC'S RESPONSIBILITY OR THE INSPECTOR'S OR THE SUPERVISOR'S. IT'S THE ENTIRE TEAM'S.

around the factory. As we began to lean out our processes, things began to visibly change and when we moved to a just-in-time production system, our inventory levels in the factory went down and this freed up the mezzanine storage areas.

At the same time, an earthquake in February 2001 destroyed the office building that our engineers worked in and we scrambled to move 1,400 engineers and support staff to temporary locations. Under normal conditions, a move of 1,400 people would have been a major undertaking, but the facilities staff pulled this off over a weekend.

These two things happening at the same time led us to think about how we could use all the assets on the site more efficiently. We asked ourselves: how do we create a way to help people work more productively, meet our vision of a leaner production system, and use the space that we have on the site better without rebuilding the engineering building?

So we started to think about moving everyone into the factory. It's something I had wanted to do since 1989, when I worked in manufacturing engineering. I frequently heard from factory workers that design engineers didn't come to the factory often enough.

Yes, you've called this "the tragedy of classical manufacturing." The tragedy of classical manufacturing is that designers are separated from assemblers. We've learned from Japanese manufacturers that there are gains when the engineers who support ongoing production live on the factory floor. If there's a problem with a product, it's not the mechanic's responsibility or the inspector's or the supervisor's. It's the entire team of people led by the engineer who designed it. If you design something you should be responsible for whether or not somebody can build it.

The real opportunity for Renton was to change the way people worked together. The idea was to bring everybody together around the product, because everything that we do here is about the plane. If we don't sell airplanes, there's really no reason for any of us to come to work each day. If we don't produce the kinds of airplanes that our customers want to keep buying, there's no future. Getting everybody's attention focused on the airplane, and on the customer associated with that airplane, was, and still is, the primary goal.

It's as easy as **1 2 3**

How did you approach the challenge of breaking this tradition of separation?
It came together through a number of different events. I had been to the Starbucks
world headquarters in Seattle and was struck by how they designed all their corporate office space to look like their retail stores. I wanted to do something similar —
to capture what we do here at Boeing and make our offices an extension of that,
a place where people really get excited about what we do.

It was clearly important never to lose sight of the fact that we couldn't create
a work environment in the factory that disenfranchised the people who had traditionally worked in the factory. We couldn't create the haves and the have-nots.
We couldn't forget that it was a factory and that we were here to build airplanes.

We used the term "industrial cool" to talk about the environment we were trying to create. We didn't want to change what was there — the steel beams and the
corrugated metal walls — we just wanted to make it livable for everyone. A key to
that was what we called "the right to light" — we punched windows into the exterior
walls to bring natural light into a space that traditionally shuts it out entirely.

So the goals were to make it a good place to come to work, a fun place, but
not different from what it had been before. It would be designed in a way that
made it acceptable for everybody to do their job, recognizing that people have
different needs.

Once the design team was in place, a pilot project was launched. How did that
idea come about? We were inspired by the idea that we had moved 1,400 engineers and support staff over a weekend. You have to work in a big company to
know how hard that would be to do if you planned it. The business of building

airplanes is cyclical and we knew that if we were going to make a big change, the best time to do it was when we were in a downturn. We created a small pilot area. It was like a model showroom. We placed notices in our internal publications so people could go and check out the space and we asked for feedback about working in an area like that. This let people know that something was going to happen that was different.

We followed that up by moving a group of 40 volunteers, all engineers, into the factory, placing them on the mezzanine with just traditional office furniture.

Did they have any kind of hesitations? They thought it was an interesting idea until the birds started flying in and landing on their desks. It wasn't an optimal situation. The lighting wasn't very good. The engineers had to walk down three flights of stairs to help the mechanics with the airplanes. At the end of a 60-day stay, we told the engineers that they could move back — and none of them wanted to leave. They all stayed and said, "This is much better," despite the conditions they were working in. It really gave us hope.

At first everybody had been sensitive to the idea that engineers wouldn't want to work in that environment. They're used to quiet cubicles, privacy, and carpets. We also learned along the way that the mechanics, who for years had said, "You know, the engineers never come to the factory to help us," were intimidated by the prospect of 1,400 engineers moving to the factory. People were moving into "their house," so they started to get nervous too. We worked very carefully to make sure that everybody knew what the expectations were and that we were being respectful of everybody's work habits.

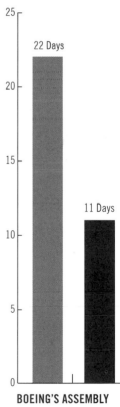

BOEING'S ASSEMBLY TIME FRAME

22 Days

11 Days

 1999, Before Lean and Renovation

 2005, After Lean and Renovation

AN AWESOME ASSEMBLY LINE

Boeing's commitment to continuous improvement in assembly processes means the workplace environment has to enable groups to reassemble as processes evolve. Early on, and throughout the design process we spent time with a cross section of individuals within the organization to better understand their current lean work practices. The goal was to develop a framework that would enable the continuing evolution of workplace culture. The framework emphasized two aspects: it's all about the plane; it's all about the people.

From virtually any place within the office environment, you never lose sight of the airplanes moving through the assembly line. The program created collaborative spaces that were always oriented towards the plane. You are simultaneously a participant and a spectator in creating the world's best airplanes. As a design team, we were inspired and in awe of the assembly process. We wanted to make this amazing and continuous transformation from parts at one end to a completed airplane at the other visually explicit. That was a critical aspect of how Boeing's vision drove our programming and design efforts. Standing in the office environment of this 1,000-foot-long, 100-foot-high building, seeing each airplane transform continuously in front of your eyes, creates a lasting and positive impression—a morale booster. It makes the familiar new once again.

Nothing said it better than Boeing family day. Families from engineering and assembly could stand back, gain perspective, share their work, and realize that we are all in this together— that they were a family.

ANNE CUNNINGHAM
Principal, NBBJ

How did you create a space that put those fears to rest for both groups? We talked extensively with NBBJ about collaboration. They developed a concept where the factory floor was treated like a showroom. They built the office-tower walls out of translucent polycarbonate panels and transparent glazing. It's very open, so one of the things that we talked about was the idea that when people sit in their cubicles or office space on these mezzanine levels looking out at the factory, it couldn't be like a fishbowl. We didn't want everyone on the floor feeling like everybody up above was staring at them. NBBJ came up with the idea of inter- spersing glass with the opaque Lexan. The light comes through it, you can see shapes, but it's not transparent like glass. There is some privacy; at the same time there's a tremendous amount of connectivity. It works well as a way of cele- brating what we do and making a direct connection between the planes and the knowledge behind them.

As people started to move into the factory over a series of months, we started to form neighborhood associations, almost like a Welcome Wagon. We made a point of bringing the engineering groups down to the factory floor, pairing them up with the people who worked on the airplane or who installed the parts that they designed. We also had the mechanics go up and see where the engineers sat. By walking into each other's space they partnered together to try to break down the barriers between them.

You started this project off with the idea that there were productivity gains that you could make, and ways in which this could work with your lean process. How have you been able to measure the achievements of this facility? We can measure the productivity gains that we've achieved through leaning out the pro- duction systems, whether it is in the white collar areas or the blue collar areas, but it's more challenging to measure if people are working together more collabo- ratively or to determine whether they are more productive.

We've been working on putting those metrics together, and we do see improve- ment. We see it in a variety of ways. The time that it takes us to resolve problems continues to get shorter and shorter. If we have a quality issue on one airplane in the factory, it will often occur on multiple airplanes—especially if it's related to a

CHANGE TOOL IN ACTION: 11
MAKE EVERYONE THE ARCHITECT
Boeing Surplus is a vast warehouse of leftovers from the factories, open to the public. The unexpected array, such as abandoned bamboo crates used for shipping airplane parts, makes a wonderful creative outlet. Seeing this lovely woven material in a different context was our genesis for incorporating Boeing products into the design.

We moved some huge templates from which airplane parts had been cut onto the site and began compositional studies. Boeing painters joined us first and then others on the floor got inspired. We provided guidelines and let them go for it. The "moonshine people" who work the two night shifts began doing really interesting pieces. All the artwork created became a design metaphor for our vision, "Parts to Whole."

ERIC LEVINE
Principal, NBBJ

part that comes from outside the company. We are correct-
ing those problems much more quickly in-line rather than
having multiple airplanes go to the factory with the same
problems. In the last three or four years, we have reduced
the number of flow days in the factory for final assembly
from 22 to 11.

*Do you have a sense of how this project has changed
Boeing itself?* I think it has changed the people who work
in Renton. They behave differently than they did before.
I think everybody who goes there recognizes that there's
something really different happening. And it's not just the
physical space, it's how people feel about what they do
and about the environment that they work in.

You can make the physical change but progress comes
from people internalizing it and then culturally changing
their behavior to complement it. That doesn't happen
overnight, but you can see that it has been happening in
Renton. People come to work and they are committed
and engaged. It's an environment where they feel like they
can make a contribution every day—and they do. ✦

GETTING EVERYBODY'S ATTENTION FOCUSED ON THE AIRPLANE, AND ON THE CUSTOMER ASSOCIATED WITH THAT AIRPLANE, WAS, AND STILL IS, THE PRIMARY GOAL.

CHANGE DESIGN

ESSAYS

Daniel Pink

Daniel Pink is the author, most recently, of A Whole New Mind, *about the rise of right-brain thinking in modern economies. His writing on work, design, and economic transformation appears in many publications, including* The New York Times, Harvard Business Review, Fast Company, *and* Wired, *where he is a contributing editor.*

What is design? I'll fall back on the easy (and perhaps simplistic) definition: design is utility combined with significance. Utility without significance is a forgettable functionality. Significance without utility is mere ornamentation.

Why does that definition matter with regard to the design of humane, productivity-enhancing workspaces? My first instinct is to say that workspaces have sacrificed one aspect of our definition on the altar of the other. What is a cubicle farm, after all, except a triumph of utility over significance? But I don't think that's fair. In my travels and reporting, I've seen many organizations that seem sincere in trying to create better work environments. There's a growing mainstream recognition that significance can enhance utility—and a realization that the most talented workers want a workspace that is more appealing and uplifting than acres of dreary cubicles sprouting from a landscape of gray carpet. I truly believe that many organizations desire to create better workplaces. The reason they fail is that they don't know how.

The reason they don't know how is because they've accepted a cheapened form of significance handed to them by the descendants of American architect Frank Lloyd Wright, who screwed his furniture to the floor of his buildings so that people didn't mess up his handiwork. Today's corporate men and women are not as aggressively disdainful of human beings as the great master was, but they're often just as woefully clueless. People matter. That's a trite sentiment, I know, but it's often neglected in the pursuit of the hip, the nifty, and the photogenic.

What, then, are the skills that matter most? Two come to mind. One skill is "boundary crossing." Many people in business are very uncomfortable crossing into different domains. Their expertise is so great in one area that they feel like amateurs in other domains—and therefore avoid them. But that approach no longer works. It's a multi-world. The rewards go to the multidisciplinary, the multilingual, the multifaceted. And if people matter (not just in the touchy-feely sense, but to the bottom line), the second key skill is empathy—seeing with someone else's eyes and feeling with someone else's heart. This is a consummate design skill, of course. But empathy is moving to the core of business—because working in outwardly beautiful buildings where people can't connect and where they can't reach their potential is not much better than being stuck in row 14, cube nine of a Dilbertian workspace. But infusing all aspects of business with greater empathy—for employees, for customers, for each other—that can change the world. Empathy is both effective and transcendent—the ultimate combination of utility and significance.

Bruce Mau

Bruce Mau is the founder and Creative Director of Bruce Mau Design Inc., a studio with international recognition for innovation across a wide range of projects achieved in collaboration with some of the world's leading architects and institutions, artists and entrepreneurs, academics and businesses. His most recent book, produced in collaboration with The Institute Without Boundaries, is Massive Change.

For me, one of the big questions is: What is the future of the workplace? Is the workplace an office or a studio? Is the workplace a place where you can spill things? If you can't spill things, you've got a problem.

We can now look with a certain amount of clarity at the 20th century and see what happened to modernity, and in some ways what happened was the Henry Ford concept of breaking things into expertise, into pieces that you could optimize.

In architecture that meant that the building became the project. But in fact, if you go back into the history of architecture, the building isn't the project. How to live— and work—is the project. So, another big question arises: How do you get from 20th century architectural practice back to more holistic thinking?

There is an arrogance in the classical understanding of design, and you can see its legacy in different fields. For instance, with every hospital you go into, the designers, it seems, were absolutely convinced it would be the last hospital ever designed; this was it, they had finally figured it out! That's because in the past century architecture has, for the most part, been conceived of as "hardware," the physical, material, fixed part of an operating system. In fact, what we now know is that architecture isn't hardware; it's software. It's a software platform that supports applications; what you're really

designing when you're designing a building is not a stable resolution but a dynamic equilibrium. To go back to my example, in hospitals you cannot know the innovation that will happen in medical science in the years to come, and you must design the platform with that in mind. You have to say, "Well, our real job is change, and supporting it in the long term." So the new hospital is version 1.0, and there will be 2.0, and 3.0. You're making something that has to hold together as a platform, but the real ambition is to sustain ongoing evolution.

It takes a lot more courage to do that than to do what most people think of when they think of architecture. It takes a totally different methodology and sensibility. One of the things to keep in mind is that everything communicates. A building tells a story without words. You're either communicating intentionally or it's like a garden hose without a sprinkler: everything will get wet eventually but it's going to be ugly. When you realize that everything is speaking, you realize an environment is talking all the time. And a lot of that talking— not only in environments but in companies generally— is mumbling and grumbling and whispered complaints. It's just under the audible tone, but it's the wrong message.

I believe that the opportunity is to make that message a song, to make it sing about value and potential and possibilities. Because holistic design methodology begins with this thought: "Anything is possible."

Jeanne Liedtka

Jeanne Liedtka is Executive Director of the Batten Institute at the University of Virginia's Darden Graduate School of Business Administration, a member of its faculty, and the author of many papers on design and business, including "In Defense of Strategy as Design" in the California Management Review.

We have much to learn from buildings that are spectacular failures — not minor, thoughtless buildings, boxes with no forethought given to them. I mean buildings that were lavishly designed but that seem to lack any facilitative connection to their ostensible purpose. These are the beautiful buildings that we admire as we pass through, buildings that seem to co-exist alongside of us but that we never really inhabit.

I know such a building. It is gorgeous, recently built on a venerable American university campus, and meant to evoke in a very literal way Thomas Jefferson's idea of the "Academical Village"—lawn, covered porticos and all. However, it is full of hallways that dead-end and separate buildings for faculty and students. Those who work there say the sense of disconnection and loss of interaction that accompanied the move into the new quarters was palpable. The old building, on the other hand, was a hideous '70s-era bunker — but it had corridors that circled, it squashed its inhabitants together, and, for those inhabitants, operated and felt like Jefferson's learning community in a way that they feel the new building, built so deliberately to look like Jefferson's, never will. It represents building as symbol, decoupled from any deep understanding of specific purpose. It is, it seems, a type of building that we all love to look at, and only discover the deficiencies of when it's time to move in.

Perhaps very little of the fault lies with the designer. If the client has no clear sense of the kind of behaviors they want their space to evoke, then it is no surprise that built environments reflect that lack of specificity. This would certainly be true of many business organizations. Consider the enormous popularity and endurance of the Dilbert-like cubicle. Was there ever a design so superficially functional and yet utterly soulless? A padded cell in exchange for the illusion of privacy and flexibility.

This desire for flexibility often takes the easy way out, settling for bland spaces that give little thought to any one purpose in their rush to accommodate many purposes. The specificity that makes great design so engaging is sacrificed. Designs endure when they get the basics — the understanding of a particular set of human needs and wants — right. That takes a level of disciplined forethought on the part of both the client and the designer that is, I suppose, rather rare, both in the world of architecture and in the world of business.

Alexi Marmot

Alexi Marmot is a London-based architect and workplace consultant. She is the founder of AMA Alexi Marmot Associates, a firm offering high-level advice to organizations with complex space and people issues. She's the author of the book Office Space Planning: Designing for Tomorrow's Workplace.

Office space is treated by many organizations as a commodity, needing little adaptation to meet the unique attributes of the company. The corporate real estate VP or facility manager selects ready-made space from a serviced office company or a speculative property developer, much as a new car or a new printer might be purchased. Standard monochrome cubicles are ordered from a building interiors contractor or major furniture manufacturer. Furniture is bought from a mail-order supplier and delivered, together with copy paper and printer cartridges. The outcome is formulaic. People "lift and shift" into the new space and carry on just as before. No one has realized that more is possible.

By contrast, other organizations seek the right and valid office space for their needs. They treat office space as an important lever to reinvent customer service, work processes, and behaviors through spatial redesign. They want to change; the new work environment is imagined then implemented and, in turn, helps drive change.

In fact, this process is a powerful spur to business change. Building changes take months to years, from drawn solution to move-in—enough time for change management on several fronts. Conversely, the overt visibility of new physical space helps to speed up change that might otherwise have happened more slowly.

When people come together in space and time, great things can happen. Yet too many office spaces breed boredom, inefficiency, and anomie; too many museums are user-unfriendly; too many schools turn people away from learning; too many hospitals breed infection; and too many cities are dysfunctional.

Converting poor environments into success stories is never easy. The successful examples work only when a series of necessary steps are followed: the goals and objectives are articulated clearly; top management buys in; physical and process changes go hand in hand; and change is introduced gradually, persistently, and eventually embraced by all.

Physical change without organizational redesign is a lost opportunity. Organizational change without changes to the physical environment is difficult and slow. Physical and organizational redesign together can help reshape our companies, our public institutions, and our urban communities. Most of the time, a "lift and shift" approach to the future is all that is asked. But if clients want "business as usual" to become "business as unusual," then integrating physical and organizational redesign is essential.

Richard Swett

Richard Swett is an architect, former US ambassador, and former congressman. He is a senior fellow of the Design Futures Council, a senior counsellor at APCO Worldwide, a global strategic communication and public relations firm, and a senior advisor at the Greenway Group, a consulting firm for the design industry. He's the author of the book Leadership by Design: Creating an Architecture of Trust.

Design's absence in many of the professions of today can be traced to two basic facts. First, education, particularly in the US, does not teach an appreciation of the design process, much less its utilization as a problem-solving tool. Second, many designers have little desire to apply their skill set to the world outside of design. These two conditions successfully keep the full benefits of design from the broader world of corporate or public governance.

I have seen communities where crossovers have been made to the benefit of both sides, but they are still few and far between. My experience as the American Ambassador to Denmark exposed me to a community that both teaches its youth an appreciation of design and employs the design process consistently in corporate and public problem-solving processes.

I argue that designers must become leaders who bridge the gap between their world and the worlds of commerce and politics because, without the educational preparation in design that is lacking in so many countries, no one is looking for the help design has to offer.

Master builders of yore understood the depth and breadth of society and how design addressed a multitude of issues. We lack this kind of integrated leadership today and although, in the United States, our cities have been built and filled, they must now contend with overcrowding, rehabilitation, renovation, security, and sustainability, to name but a few issues. These are issues that need to be managed by someone with a master builder's eye.

Leaders of today's corporate world come out of an education based on case study. Lawyers share the same experience. In the political world many leaders are the offspring of special interest groups and come to positions of power limited by a narrow vision. The threats to the world can only be solved by an inclusive leadership that integrates all facets of the global community to work harmoniously toward finding solutions. On the economic, environmental, and health fronts business is going to play an important role and will require the vision of the master builder possessed by the designer. Therefore, leadership by design is a must.

IT TAKES A VILLAGE TO MAP A GENE

By mirroring its setting, Wellcome Trust's Sanger Institute weaves rural cues through its high-tech research campus, encouraging creative and collaborative science.

THE WELLCOME TRUST SANGER INSTITUTE IS ONE OF THE WORLD'S PRE-EMINENT GENOME RESEARCH CENTERS. IT IS BEST KNOWN AS THE SINGLE LARGEST CONTRIBUTOR TO THE GLOBAL HUMAN GENOME PROJECT.

FUNDING IS PRIMARILY PROVIDED BY THE WELLCOME TRUST, EUROPE'S LARGEST BIOMEDICAL RESEARCH CHARITY WITH INVESTMENTS OF $20 BILLION.

THE INSTITUTE STUDIES THE GENOMES OF ORGANISMS RANGING FROM HUMANS TO MICE, FISH, WORMS, AND YEASTS, AS WELL AS PATHOGENS THAT CAUSE DISEASES SUCH AS MALARIA (AFFECTING ABOUT 400 MILLION PEOPLE EACH YEAR), SLEEPING SICKNESS (ABOUT TWO MILLION CASES EACH YEAR), TYPHOID (ABOUT 17 MILLION CASES EACH YEAR), AND TUBERCULOSIS (ABOUT NINE MILLION CASES EACH YEAR).

THE INSTITUTE'S CANCER GENOME PROJECT IS AMONG THE WORLD'S LARGEST CANCER GENOME STUDIES. IT SEARCHES FOR GENETIC MUTATIONS THAT CAUSE THE MOST COMMON CANCERS, INCLUDING BREAST, LUNG, COLORECTAL, OVARIAN, AND PROSTATE.

LOCATED ON A 125-ACRE (51-HECTARE) CAMPUS IN HINXTON, CAMBRIDGE, THE EXISTING LABS ACCOMMODATED 650 STAFF. THIS 27,000-SQUARE-METER (291,000-SQUARE-FOOT) CAMPUS EXTENSION ALLOWS THE INSTITUTE TO ADD UP TO 200 MORE SCIENTISTS.

IN ITS FIRST SEVEN YEARS, THE STAFF SIZE OF THE SANGER INSTITUTE INCREASED FROM 15 TO 580. EIGHTY PERCENT OF THE STAFF LIVE WITHIN 16 KILOMETERS (10 MILES) OF THE CAMPUS, ALTHOUGH THEY ARE RECRUITED FROM MORE THAN 20 COUNTRIES AROUND THE WORLD.

THE PROJECT INCLUDES A MASTER PLAN FOR THE EXTENDED CAMPUS. DEVELOPMENT IS PLANNED IN THREE PHASES. THE FIRST INCLUDES AN EXPANSION TO SANGER INSTITUTE ACADEMIC/LABORATORY BUILDINGS, A SUPER-COMPUTING DATA CENTER AND CAMPUS AMENITIES. FUTURE PHASES INCLUDE AN INNOVATION CENTER FOR STARTUP BUSINESSES AND FACILITIES FOR SPIN-OFFS.

THE SUSTAINABLE CAMPUS ACHIEVED THE UK GREEN MEASUREMENT INSTITUTE, BREEAM, EQUIVALENT OF AN "EXCELLENT" RATING FOR SCIENCE FACILITIES.

JOHN COOPER
DIRECTOR OF RESOURCES, WELLCOME TRUST

John Cooper is Director of Resources for the Wellcome Trust in London, UK, and is also Managing Director of the Wellcome Trust Genome Campus near Cambridge, UK. He is responsible for a wide range of business services, including HR, IT, and Facilities Management as well as several large capital projects, including the Genome Campus expansion. He also manages the Wellcome Trust Conference Centres on the Genome Campus and in London, and an interesting and fast-growing program of advanced genomics training courses for post-doctoral researchers. Before joining the Trust in 1999 Cooper spent 30 years in the commercial electronics industry, formerly as a main board director of a UK public company with extensive business interests in the USA and Europe.

Let's start by talking about Wellcome Trust itself. We are a research funding organization. Particularly in the UK, a lot of people remember that there was a drug company called Wellcome or Glaxo-Wellcome, and we were confused with them regularly, so we always make the point that we're a charitable foundation, not a drug company. We fund research, mainly research carried out in universities and research institutes. For instance, we're the major non-US funder of the Human Genome Project. We fund a lot of research into tropical medicine, malaria and HIV/AIDS, and tuberculosis, and a lot of basic blue-sky biological research, often in the UK universities. Our goal is the public good; our mission is to promote research with the aim of improving human and animal health.

You are dedicated not just to research, but also to applied research. Yes, we do some applied research—probably not as much as we would like to. We take the view that we should not try to do what the commercial world can do as well or better, but there are gaps in the process of translating fundamental research into healthcare benefits that we believe we can fill. Usually it's very early-stage investment in promising ideas. When the market is ready to take them up, then we pull out.

You mentioned the Wellcome Trust involvement in the Human Genome Project, and you are chief executive of the Wellcome Trust Genome Campus. Can you recap the role that Wellcome Trust has played in the Human Genome Project?
Through the Wellcome Trust Sanger Institute, we funded about 35 percent of the international effort on the Human Genome Project. The other major contribution we made is our insistence that the results of the research be published immediately, so that whatever sequence had been discovered during the day was put on the Internet that evening. We insisted that if we were to be involved in the project the results had to be made freely available to scientists anywhere in the world. And that, of course, goes straight to our mission.

Can you describe the original campus where that work was done? Until, I think, about the Second World War, it was a country estate, Hinxton Hall, an 18th century country house with 125 acres of land.

During the war, Hinxton Hall was used by the US Air Force as accommodation for pilots from the nearby US air base at Duxford. After the war it was converted into a research center by a British engineering group. They pulled out. It was lying unused and not in great condition in the early 1990s, when we were looking for somewhere to start up work on the Human Genome Project. So, we bought it. Initially people worked out of the old buildings, and then in the mid-1990s we built some new laboratories.

Wellcome Trust first applied to expand the campus in the late 1990s. What was the original intent? The original purpose, actually, was to build an innovation center and some grow-on spaces for small genomics companies, the idea being to develop a science park around the genomics facility. And we were unable to get planning consent for that, after many public inquiries. In the meantime, we came under increasing pressure for space for academic research facilities, so we had a change of plan. We split the project into two parts. Phase One was to build more academic space. Phase Two would be to build the innovation center—or incubator, as everyone calls it—and commercial space.

So far, all we have done is build the academic space. The world has moved on and the biotech sector is not doing particularly well. So, we're waiting until we believe that there's a reasonable demand for genomics start-up activities before we make a decision on building Phase Two.

What motivated the opposition that you talked about to the original plans?
I think it was concern about development in greenfield sites. Cambridge is an area that has grown very fast (by UK standards, not by the standards of Silicon Valley) and the infrastructure has not kept pace, so there are problems with roads and schools—perceived problems; probably nothing compared to some major US cities, or indeed London. But Cambridge is a very beautiful university city in a very pleasant rural area, nice rolling countryside, and a lot of people wanted to keep it that way. I live in that area myself, so in many ways I agree with them.

But, in point of fact, when we went back with our revised proposal, which was four to five years on from the original proposal, we had no problem. There'd been a lot of local debate, a lot of discussion between ourselves and the planning

CAMBRIDGE IS A VERY BEAUTIFUL
UNIVERSITY CITY IN A VERY
PLEASANT RURAL AREA,
NICE ROLLING COUNTRYSIDE,
AND A LOT OF PEOPLE WANTED
TO KEEP IT THAT WAY.

MOST BRITISH SCIENCE IS CARRIED OUT IN UNIVERSITIES OR IN CITY CENTERS, OFTEN IN OLD BUILDINGS. WE'VE CREATED A LOVELY RURAL CAMPUS WITH MODERN BUILDINGS.

authorities, and I have to say that the planning authorities and the local community were very cooperative. I think what had happened in the meantime was people had seen the tremendous achievements of the Sanger Institute and the Human Genome Project and they actually felt proud to be associated with it. Five years before that, of course, it was a bit of an unknown, and it was going to be a very commercial development. Now it was a research development to take further work of which the local communities themselves had become justifiably proud.

How did those initial concerns of the surrounding communities influence the design approach? We tried to make sure that the buildings were as unobtrusive as possible, so they're low buildings, maximum two stories. The two biggest buildings have green roofs, and the roofs slope down towards one of the villages, so if the residents are looking at the site from where they live what they actually see is a plant called sedum—they see a large sedum roof, they see flowers.

So that was one response. Another response was to make sure that what we did had a positive environmental impact. Around the edge of the site is a small river that flooded regularly, and there was concern that the runoff from new buildings might exacerbate those problems. We built a 15-acre wetland, so that when the river overflowed it flowed into this wetland, which we turned into a nature reserve. It's only been operating for about a year, but already otters have returned to breed in the area, and some interesting birds. It will take five to 10 years to reach anything like maturity, but when it does it will be a very nice small nature reserve.

We also tried to use materials for the buildings that fitted with the local style, so, for instance, a number of the walls of the buildings are made of flint stones embedded in concrete panels so it looks like a flint wall, which there are a lot of in the local villages.

As much as possible we built underground parking. The surface car parking is hidden behind grass banks with trees and shrubs on the top. So, we've tried to make the buildings blend in with the local environment.

Obviously these features have a tremendous effect on people who are outside the campus. Do they affect the people who are on the campus? As you can imagine, working in 125 acres of parkland, there's a very nice working environment. Most

RURAL ROOTS

Touchstones act as a reference, a criterion guiding, directing and focusing a design team's efforts. The inspiration for this tool came from Cirque du Soleil. When they put on a production, they come up with an initial concept, and as they start to do their lighting design, their set design, their choreography, their acts, everything has to support that one concept. If it doesn't, it's thrown out. You get stronger design that way. You're never caught in a situation where someone's saying, "Well, I just did it because I like it that way." Everything's supporting a general concept that supports the project.

On Wellcome Trust, the Number One rule was to take cues from the landscape and the area. Secondary was the idea that where you had people-focused functions, those environments were going to take their cues from nature, and where the focus of the work was more scientific in nature, those areas were going to be more man-made.

By coming up with that concrete set of rules from the very beginning, every time a question would arise about how to treat a certain area, you could always go back to that concept and say, "Okay, this is what to do." It was great for the design team and for the user groups, because when anyone said, "Why are we doing it that way?" the reply was "Remember our concept. This is how these things are ordered."

JONATHAN WARD
Principal, NBBJ

British science is carried out in universities or in city centers, and often in pretty old buildings. The environment that we've created is of a lovely rural campus with classy modern buildings on it. It certainly makes me feel good to go there.

The other thing that we've done is we've built the Cairns Pavilion, which has a new staff restaurant and a small sports hall. You can use it to play badminton and other things. We also have built a new football [soccer] pitch—very important in the UK. So we've gone a long way to improve the facilities for people, and already we've seen a big increase in the use of these facilities. The takings in the staff restaurant have shot up compared with what we had before, simply because it's a nice place.

And what are you hoping the spin-off effects will be in terms of people's creativity and productivity? What one always hopes is that by encouraging interaction between researchers working in different groups you get a cross-fertilization of ideas. You've got groups of people doing very basic science, and you've got other groups of people studying particular disease types, and clearly one hopes that these people are swapping notes and learning from each other. I don't know whether we've got any evidence, yet, that that's happened, but that's certainly one of our objectives: by encouraging informal interaction between people to improve the creativity of the place.

There is a lot of evidence that organizations that work informally work better. I'm speaking to you from our head office in London, which we've just finished, and we moved from having half our staff working in cellular offices to having all but 10 or 12 people working in open offices, and already the level of interaction has increased incredibly because, you know, they can now see and meet each other. And it's the same process in the case of the campus applied to a research environment.

As part of the expansion you had to do some recruiting from amongst the world's top scientists. How do you design and build for that sort of need? What we did first of all, of course, was to work with the people who were already there. We built good laboratory space but we built to a standard approach. Then, of course, as the new scientists started appearing, the space had to be customized, and so we were building and customizing almost at the same time. Which is fine; the way the whole project was designed and procured gave us that flexibility. So we started off not really knowing exactly what would be needed by many of the scientists, and then gradually adjusted the design along the way to give them what they needed.

On the subject of how things can be adjusted as you go along, you mentioned that the second phase of the project at this point is on hold, pending developments in the wider world. How will you be able to move on to that second phase if you need to? What we built in the first phase is actually six different buildings, and with our master plan we would put up new additional buildings on land which is immediately adjacent to what we've already built. It's easy to expand.

In some ways this new campus is an experiment in a new way of working, and that seems fitting for a scientific institute, but what made it an experiment that you felt was worth undertaking? Well, I suppose two things. You really do have to believe that the quality of work that you're doing there is important, and I think everybody believes that the work that was done on the Human Genome Project, the work that's now going on, is really high quality and very important. Secondly, you have to believe that creative people can spark ideas off each other if you put them together in the sort of environment where they can have relatively casual interaction with each other. And that all seems right, it seems sensible, it doesn't seem far-fetched to believe that creative people working together will generate good ideas, so it's a matter of building an environment which facilitates that. You can't make it happen, but you can build something that will allow it to happen. So I suppose it's a bit of an act of faith, but it seems a pretty good bet. ✦

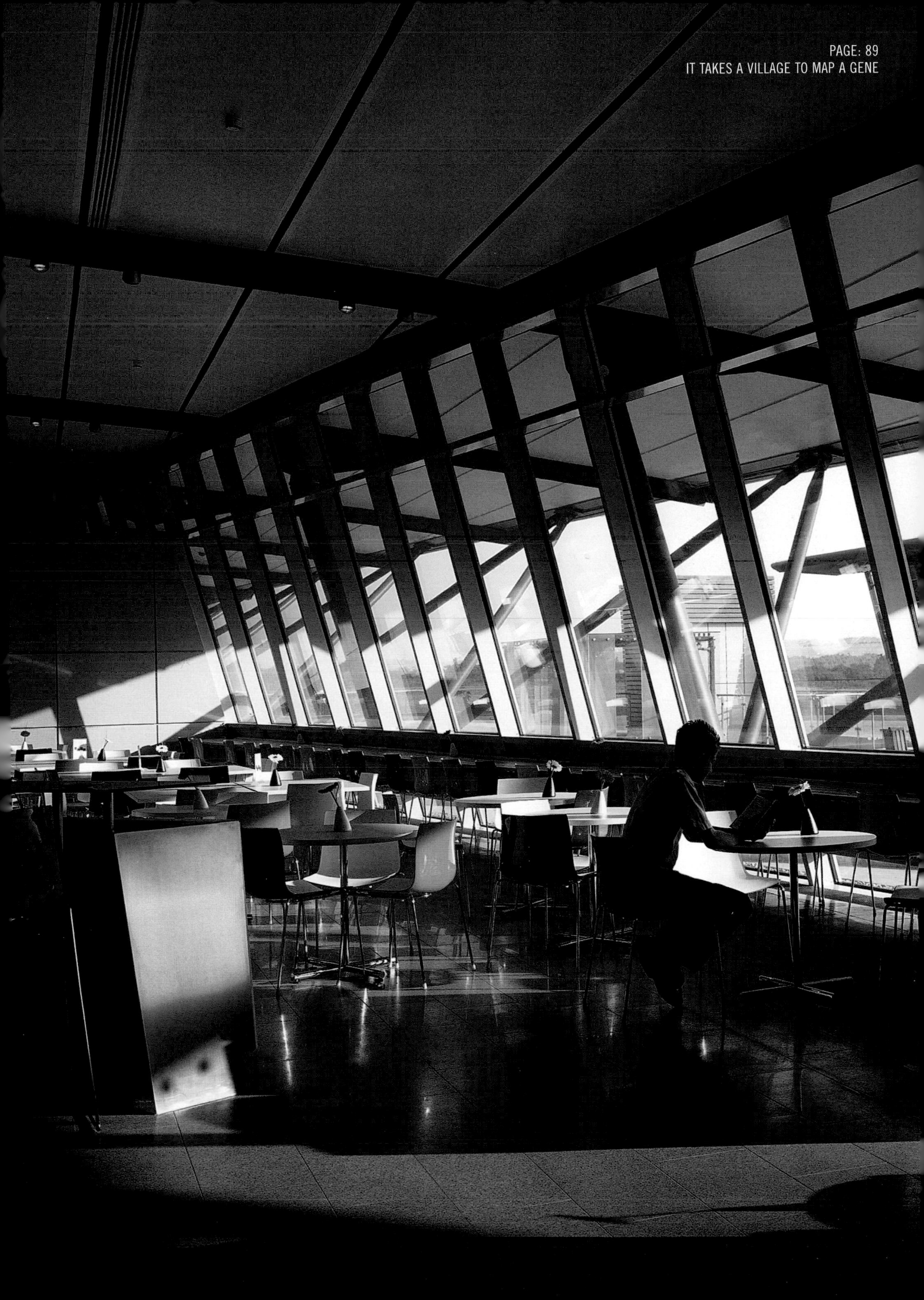

ALLAN BRADLEY
DIRECTOR, WELLCOME TRUST SANGER INSTITUTE

You took over as Director of the Sanger Institute at about the same time as the project to expand the campus began. What were your initial thoughts about the project, especially in relation to what you hoped to do as director? When I arrived, this campus had a very single, clear mission, which was decoding the human genome. The mission that is unfolding now is about not just understanding what all those letters encode but what that code really means, so it's about the function of genes.

And so from a campus that deployed a single technology—genome sequencing—it's now going to be a campus that has a much more diverse infrastructure need. So that meant more high-spec space in terms of molecular biology, more space for animal experiments, and a lot more space for a computing infrastructure.

What you're doing has been described as bringing biology to the genome. You know, some people refer to the genome as the book of life, but what you have to remember is that it is a book with a million pages of text when printed out, and so what we need to do is understand what is on those pages and what it is there for: why is that sequence there, what happens if something goes wrong, how is it important in health, and how is it important in disease? Just having information is extremely important, but you have to go beyond, you have to use it.

And so our mission is really two-fold. We are adding value to that sequence, or bringing biology to the genome, if you like, but we also are sharing that information with the community at large. A very big part of our mission—and has been from the start—is giving away information about the sequence, helping people do their experiments on-line using our computer infrastructure, and sharing data we generate ourselves with external users as well.

How equipped were you to be able to take those next steps within the original campus? In some ways we were extremely restricted. For example, even when this building, the Sulston

PHIL BUTCHER
HEAD OF INFORMATION TECHNOLOGY, WELLCOME TRUST SANGER INSTITUTE

You're Head of IT for the Sanger Institute. What's the importance of Information Technology in this type of scientific setting? The Sanger Institute has been, for the past 13 years, pretty much devoted to sequencing human DNA, which is made up of three billion base pairs or chemicals. End to end they are very similar in each human, and a very small fraction are different, which gives us different color eyes, height, hair, and so on. Our whole aim was to take human DNA and be able to put the sequence of chemicals in a row so you could read, from one end to the other, the three billion base pairs. The chemicals are adenine, cytosine, thiamine, and guanine, which is computationally represented by A, C, T, and G, so what we have to do is get those As, Cs, Ts, and Gs and put them in the right order for three billion characters made up of just those four bases.

So, do the math! It's a huge computational effort to do that in the first place. But it's been achieved. Since we started this endeavor in 1993–94, the Sanger Institute has contributed more and more complete DNA to the public domain database than any other organization in the world.

Now we're sequencing other genomes, of other organisms like zebra fish and mice. We have 10 to 20 genomes available on our web site, so one can be compared with the other to find differences and similarities, so that we can understand how humans are made up, which inevitably will lead us into understanding how we can apply that to medicine, and how we can treat particular hereditary diseases.

One of the main goals of the institute's new campus is to better enable data emerging from the genome work to be translated into practical health benefits. How can data processing help achieve that goal? Much of the science now depends on the computational side to analyze the data. If you have three billion base pairs—and that's just one genome—and you want to compare it to another genome, that's three billion against three billion base pairs. You can't do that without very high-scale, high-performance computers.

CHANGE TOOL IN ACTION: 04
SITE SEE

The site is extremely delicate. The Cambridgeshire environment is mostly agricultural; Cambridge itself is a 20-minute drive away. There are other developments, including laboratories being built in the countryside, and there's a lot of concern from the local villages to slow down the spread of development and not let it completely change the landscape. The design team took that as a cue and asked: What can we do to make this building fit onto the site? It's a very open site; you can see it from far away because it's flat. There are hills surrounding one side and a small village on the other side. The team spent a lot of time talking about the concept of cutting into the landscape and slipping the building into those cuts, so the landscape would mask the very technical parts of the building. We wanted the people parts to be as open as possible, but as you moved away from that you could start digging into the earth, blocking the bulk of the building from view from the village.

JONATHAN WARD
Principal, NBBJ

Laboratories, I'm in was built and finished—in 1996, I think—they had significantly underestimated the requirement for the computing infrastructure in order to deliver information to the world.

The design for the new campus is very different from what has been on the grounds up until now. How did Sanger scientists initially view the design concept? We were heavily consulted and heavily involved in the design at all levels, including answering questions about whether we wanted it to be a single building or multiple buildings. Obviously, most of the ideas were brought to us by the architects, but they were bounced off us in a series of meetings, to make sure that we and the architects and engineers really truly agreed as to what we were trying to build.

What were some of the key ideas that came up through that consultative process? Well, I think one of the things they wanted to do was move the heart

of the campus a little bit away from where it was, so the key thing was to build a building where people in the new buildings would interact with the people in the existing building. For an institute it's very important that different groups of people know what is going on in different areas of the research enterprise; there's a lot of science that is nucleated by casual connection—you know, sitting down and having a cup of coffee, or bumping into one another in the hall or in an open space somewhere. And it's actually quite hard, I think, to make that happen when we're spread out over quite a lot of space. The new building, I think, really has enabled that to occur not only within the groups in the building, but also between the people in that building and other parts of the campus.

There's an area of the new campus called the market square. How does that function? The market square is a space between the cafeteria, the coffee shop, and the sports facility on

So in some essential way, the computational work is the science, or is a large part of the science? Exactly. It's an integral part. Genomic-based science cannot be done without a very decent computational infrastructure.

Over the years, we have grown a very large, high-performance computing infrastructure—300,000 gigabytes. If you think, in your PC you may have a 40 gigabyte disk. We have thousands of CPUs working on these problems. We've had up to 400 machines in a rack, and when you have that much computer power in a single space, not only does it draw a lot of power, but it also outputs an awful lot of heat. You can't just switch these things on in an office and hope for the best. It means you need a radical design for how you're going to deal with these heat loads. The idea of providing a computer room is a very, very serious business for us.

Given what you've been talking about, it's interesting that when you were asked what you would like in a new data center—or computer room, to put it simply—you specified a computing

capacity that was, per square meter, still two to three times greater than the industry standard. Why were you setting your sights so high? Our main problem is that we always outgrow the environment. The industry in general hasn't been able to build systems that are really future-proof for a good, long while.

You have to take into consideration as well the differences between machine rooms in the US and machine rooms in the UK and Europe. In the US, where space is easier to come by, people tend to build larger machine rooms, and therefore the power, heat, and density problems are less. In the UK and Europe, where we don't have so much free space, the parcels of land we're given to build on tend to be smaller. We are trying to do very high capacity computing on a smaller footprint. Therefore, the heat and power density problems are more relevant to us.

The new campus has many elements to it but the data center was determined to be the riskiest part of the entire project. Why was that? There were a lot of unknowns. Originally, the design

CHANGE TOOL IN ACTION: 10
INVEST IN TRAVEL
John Cooper asked the team what the riskiest part of the project was. "Well, the riskiest part of this project is the data center, because it has to stay live, and it's big and it's powerful." It's well above normal design criteria. The team was talking about going to look at some new cooling systems in the United States, and John Cooper said, "If you guys think this is risky, we'd better get out there, go visit them and make sure we know what we're getting ourselves into."

BRUCE NEPP
Principal, NBBJ

FOR A RESEARCH INSTITUTE IT'S VERY IMPORTANT THAT DIFFERENT GROUPS OF PEOPLE KNOW WHAT'S GOING ON IN DIFFERENT AREAS OF THE ENTERPRISE. A LOT OF SCIENCE IS NUCLEATED BY CASUAL CONNECTION — SITTING DOWN AND HAVING A CUP OF COFFEE.

one side, and the offices of the research building on the other. Behind it are the research buildings and the supercomputing data center. And then to one side is the existing Sanger Building, now called the Sulston Laboratories. So in terms of its location it's not quite a quadrant, but the view was that it would be a place where paths would cross and connect—you know, the market square. And in fact the entrance to the carpark comes right

out in the middle of the market square, so that's another dimension that was designed to make people meet each other in the morning, because you would see people going for coffee, or going into the buildings, or going to the gym or whatever. There's nobody selling vegetables or anything like that! It's just kind of a meeting place. And people do meet casually and, if the weather's fine, they'll even stand out and discuss things. So it's a little bit like an Italian piazza.

That idea of science coming out of casual interaction, is that an accepted truth in the scientific community?
I think it is, absolutely, yes. I think you see it in modern science buildings, and also you see it in the old ones. If you go into the old science buildings in Cambridge, that meeting place is actually the tea room. Now, it's not often built into an American science building, a tea room. So they tend to build smaller little casual areas. But the cafeteria never really compensates for a tea room.

What is the tea room at Cambridge?
Well, in any academic building in Cambridge there'll be a tea room where tea and coffee are served in the morning at 10:30 and tea is served at 3:30 in the afternoon, and people will gather for a tea break. You can go to a room where most of the occupants of the building will be at that period in time, and so you can actually get a lot

CHANGE TOOL IN ACTION: 03
KEEP YOUR EYES ON THE PRIZE
The idea was to create an informal community of buildings, much like a village with a market square. You could have done a collegiate environment, a formal Gothic campus where you had the church on one end and the school of medicine on the other, with very formal forecourts and all that. But the vision emphasized a more informal approach to the campus, much more a place where people would just be walking from shop to shop, if you will, like in a village. As a result, different entities are all around the perimeter of the square like little shops, with lots of transparency between buildings, so you can see people coming in and out from office to dining to the sports facilities.

JONATHAN WARD
Principal, NBBJ

was to look at traditional computer room air conditioning units. While that's the regular way of cooling machine rooms, it's not necessarily, in our opinion, the most cost-effective or efficient way to do it these days. Early on in the project, we went to review other data centers around the world and in the US to see what technologies they were using, and we came across fan coil technology, which is what we eventually deployed, modified to fit our needs.

You mentioned the tour that you went on. One of the major epiphanies of the project occurred on a plane ride between data centers. What happened? We spent quite a lot of time in the air between various cities in order to look at these installations. So it did end up as an awful lot of time in airplane gangways, discussing on scraps of paper and laptops, with all of us pitching in and coming up with ideas about what would and wouldn't be workable.

It hasn't been widely used elsewhere, particularly in this way, so we set up room simulations using "computational fluid dynamic modeling" (CFD), and then actually built real setups that were doing research to see whether it was valid for us to go ahead. Yes, it was very risky, but we took the steps to prove the technology. We were reasonably comfortable with what we'd seen and what we could do, but the actual proving of it had to be done in parallel with the machine room being built.

We'd decided that we were going to build four quadrants, or four machine rooms, so that we could actually isolate some of the kit, rather than just building one big, 1,000-square-meter room.

One of the ideas that we came up with on the plane was that we should keep one of the four machine rooms empty so that if I do outgrow the environment we could actually refurbish the technology in there to accommodate machines that have yet to be invented.

CHANGE TOOL IN ACTION: 17
DESIGN ON THE FLY

We were being asked if Sanger's computing design load was realistic. On our US trip to visit different facilities, talk started among the team in the aisles of the airplane about the growth pattern of the Sanger. How do you justify what you need for the data center? How often will the hardware change?

So the laptops came out and we started quizzing Phil Butcher: "When you started, what was your computer processing load (MIPS)?" We tracked three different historical points, up until the design time in 2002, and came up with logarithmic growth that suggested that within 24 months of opening they could run out of capacity in the data center.

The team came to the realization that the question was "how do you get more capacity?" And of course you could hear John Cooper saying, "You're not spending another penny more."

So we quickly deduced that our only option was the innovative cooling solution, which in turn allowed us to double the computational processing capacity.

BRUCE NEPP
Principal, NBBJ

It isn't the "Eureka!" in the bathtub, or the guy with a microscope anymore. These problems are so complicated they take teams of people and huge computers.

BRAD LEATHLEY
Principal, NBBJ

of business done in that 20 minutes, rather than trading phone calls and e-mails and that kind of stuff. So it's casual, but it's not casual in terms of what it's delivering, which is important information exchange between individuals.

And have you been able to replicate that with the new facilities? Yes, and indeed in the old ones. In fact, when the architects first came here they recognized one of the successes of the current building was that there was a very popular tea room that was called The DiNA. And so they've built a similar sort of coffee bar, the Pebble Cafe, in the new building as another nucleus for people to gather.

You are just newly into the building, but can you see evidence of it working? Oh, yes. I can see it working. But one of the other aspects of the design is rather than having labs with walls, the laboratory space is a very open plan, so there are different groups who are literally back to back, whereas in previous buildings they would have had walls

dividing them up. So it means that information is flowing, because people are almost in the same space, if you like; they're sharing the lab and they're sharing the materials and they're sharing ideas.

And that comes back to things like how we deal with our data, how we share our data. We can have a bigger impact than people who do their experiments in their laboratories and then eventually put them into the scientific literature. Because we do that immediately, we have a much bigger impact, we think, than people who are more secretive about the work they're doing. And the building does support that way of working. You know, buildings without walls don't lend to secrecy.

How unusual is it to have the kind of transparency you're describing, in a lab environment? I think it's relatively unusual. When I was working in the States, there were no labs in the States that I was aware of that were built that way, certainly not in Baylor [Baylor College of Medicine, Houston, Texas], where I was previously. They'd built a

I'm not going to fill all these rooms at day one, and I have to build capacity in for expansion; otherwise, what's the point of building? If you're going to put spare capacity in, why not actually build the spare capacity? Why don't you just put the shell in and leave us the maximum amount of flexibility that we could possibly hope to have? It's what I call "the fallow field principle."

It's interesting to think of that agricultural terminology applied in such a highly technical environment. It seems suitable for a campus that is right in the middle of a pastoral area. It's true. I went to bed one night on the trip and woke up, and I thought, it's obvious. People have done this in ancient agricultural terms for years. Why not deploy this within our setting? I have a rotating crop. My crop just happens to be IT.

And actually, we save money, because we haven't filled a quarter of the building, which probably we may well have done, had we gone for the traditional method. But we decided to do this thing. So it saved money, it gave us future proofing, real future proofing

and flexibility. It has yet to be proven, but we're quietly confident.

One of your other major challenges, as you touched on earlier, was heat and cooling. In the course of figuring out how you were going to solve that, the design team talked about sticking an ice cube on top of the computers — another metaphor. What did it turn into? Well, originally the idea was that we were going to have one floor of computer rooms, and the two floors above it were going to be full of the air conditioning systems. It was going to take a huge amount of space, so it became nicknamed "the ice cube," because we had this huge, square block sitting on top of a very thin layer of machines underneath.

But of course what happened was that we moved to this fan coil system, which was installed within the machine rooms, so we could actually reorder the space that we had upstairs. Now, not only do I have an empty fourth quadrant, I actually have spare capacity within the plant rooms upstairs so that if I want to I can put in an additional

lot of labs over the 15 years I was there, but they never embraced the open-lab concept. People tended to like to have four walls and a door they could lock at night, whereas here that's impossible because the space is shared with lots of other people.

And given that it was a bit different, how did people feel about the open-lab concept when it was originally introduced? Initially, there was a little bit of trepidation about moving into that environment, but I've heard many people say to me, just in the past month, "It's amazing. Our productivity's increased since we've moved." Considering one is moving into a new building, with all of the upset that causes, just getting things organized, it's quite interesting that they already feel a positive impact.

It has also allowed a lot of flexibility in terms of managing the space, which was the other primary reason for doing it. If you're putting up walls, eventually you're going to have to take them down or move them, and we didn't want to have to deal with that. So it's very modular, it can be shifted around, benches can be taken out and other things can be put in if necessary. It's designed with flexibility—long-term flexibility—in mind.

Which is something that would be important given the way the institute is shifting its interest? Yes. Certainly my view is that science doesn't stand still, and shouldn't stand still. It'll move and we should move with it. ✦

chiller plant to accommodate the fourth room. We really do have a huge amount of flexibility in that bit we called the ice cube. To top it off, they did put blue glass all around the outside of the building, so it does look a bit like an ice cube.

It's interesting how metaphors have a way of influencing physicality. What are the effects of having a building that creates so much heat actually look like an ice cube? I think what it does do, actually — because it would normally be concrete — you only have to look at the building, and you suddenly realize how much effort it takes to cool modern day computer systems. They don't all just sit in offices. It does give an impression, I guess, to the outside world, of the kind of efforts we have to go to to support the science that we do. ✦

FINE GROUND

Starbucks World Headquarters, Seattle, 1997.

When we began the company we were really product-driven but over time we realized the business we were in was way beyond coffee. The environment was as important as the coffee, because we're in the business of human connection.

HOWARD SCHULTZ
Chairman, Starbucks

The stores themselves began to be a third place between home and work, and as a result of that we became very aware of the competitive advantage of creating very comfortable settings for customers.

H.S.

The graphic interpretation of the logo, the color of the walls — everything is done for a reason. Not to sell more goods but to sweep you into an oasis when you walk through the door. That is a designed experience.

H.S.

e company recognizes how important
e visual communication of Starbucks
s been. Whether they are working
 the warehouse floor, roasting coffee,
 as an administrative assistant,
ople feel very strongly about the voice
 Starbucks.

Starbucks has done a brilliant job of managing, through all their growth, to keep the beans and the bean counters very close together.

SCOTT WYATT
Partner, NBBJ

We're very sensitive about being a large, ubiquitous company—we don't want to be a faceless chain of stores. We have to keep dialing it down to the lowest common denominator, using design as a mechanism.

H.S.

We tried to design the headquarters around the idea of the individual's experience in the company, so that each person understood, "Ah, I work for a great world-changing brand, and yet I'm not a speck."

H.S.

NBBJ deserves a tremendous amount of credit for not only interpreting the culture and values of the company, but being able to create and design spaces for our headquarters that are mirror images of the look and feel of the culture of the company—and also of our stores. I can't tell you how many people visit this office who, when they walk through here, feel like they have just walked through a Starbucks store.

H.S.

tying their office space to their stores,
...d their stores to their graphic design
...d packaging, having one inform the
...er, Starbucks is using design to
...egrate.
...

3,500 people work in this building, and
the people who are not working for a
store but for other departments are constantly reminded of what we stand for. I
don't want to say more productive, but
people are more inspired.

H.S.

Productivity is a symptom of being
inspired. Productivity and creativity are
symptoms of people being inspired
and fulfilled and saying, "I like this."
S.W.

SWIMMING UPSTREAM

How the state, the university, the college, and the town came together to beat the odds and create a two-institution, ridge-top campus that serves students, respects residents, and restores a Washington wetland.

IN THE 1990S, WASHINGTON STATE'S HIGHER EDUCATION COORDINATING BOARD (HECB) IDENTIFIED A NEED FOR TWO NEW HIGHER EDUCATION INSTITUTIONS IN THE GROWING EXURBIA OF SEATTLE—CITIES LIKE BELLEVUE, REDMOND, BOTHELL, AND WOODINVILLE.

THE UNIVERSITY OF WASHINGTON (UW) AND THE STATE BOARD FOR COMMUNITY AND TECHNICAL COLLEGES (SBCTC) BEGAN SEPARATE SEARCHES, BUT AFTER UW ENCOUNTERED OBSTACLES IN FINDING APPROPRIATE SITES, THE HECB RECOMMENDED THAT THE TWO ENTITIES SHARE A CAMPUS.

THE TRULY FARM SITE IN BOTHELL WAS SELECTED TO BE THE COMBINED HOME OF A BRANCH CAMPUS OF THE UNIVERSITY OF WASHINGTON FOR UPPER DIVISION UNDERGRADUATE AND GRADUATE STUDENTS, AND A NEWLY CREATED COMMUNITY COLLEGE, CASCADIA COMMUNITY COLLEGE.

IN ADDITION TO CO-LOCATING THE SCHOOLS, THE PROJECT INCLUDED THE LARGEST WETLANDS RESTORATION PROJECT EVER ACCOMPLISHED IN THE STATE OF WASHINGTON.

THE TWO SCHOOLS HAVE SEPARATE FACULTIES, CLASSROOMS, AND LABORATORIES BUT SHARE A LIBRARY, BOOKSTORE, PARKING, AND FOOD SERVICE.

THE INITIAL COST OF COMBINING TWO INSTITUTIONS ON ONE CAMPUS SAVED 15 PERCENT OF THE ESTIMATED COST OF CREATING TWO SEPARATE CAMPUSES, AND IS EXPECTED TO YIELD LIFE-CYCLE COST SAVINGS OF 10 PERCENT OVER THE 25-YEAR PLANNING HORIZON. DESIGN AND CONSTRUCTION METHODS YIELDED AN ADDITIONAL $6.5 MILLION RETURN TO THE STATE'S COFFERS.

UW AND CASCADIA TOGETHER SERVE OVER 2,800 STUDENTS, 58 PERCENT OF WHOM ARE ENROLLED FULL-TIME.

EIGHTY PERCENT OF THE STUDENTS ATTEND SCHOOL WHILE WORKING AND NEARLY HALF WORK FULL-TIME. OVER 40 PERCENT ARE FIRST GENERATION COLLEGE STUDENTS.

IN FALL 2006, UW BOTHELL WILL INCREASE ENROLLMENT, WELCOMING LOWER DIVISION STUDENTS TO THE CAMPUS. UW BOTHELL ANTICIPATES ENROLLING 475 FRESHMEN AND SOPHOMORES AND ADDING MORE THAN 2,000 SEATS FOR TRANSFER STUDENTS BY THE YEAR 2010.

JIM REED

ACTING DIRECTOR OF FISCAL POLICY, WASHINGTON STATE HIGHER EDUCATION COORDINATING BOARD

Jim Reed has been with the Washington State Higher Education Coordinating Board for 17 years, during which time he has had the unique opportunity to work with state policy-makers in authorizing, planning, and developing new higher education campuses and resources. His work in this area reflects his academic background and interests in organizational behavior and planning. Based on his studies of public policy at Harvard University, Reed developed a keen interest in understanding how public policy can be effectively used as the basis for achieving excellence in complex planning and development activities. Prior to his work at the Higher Education Coordinating Board, Reed served under two Washington Governors as their Capital Budget Officer. He also served as Washington's Director of State Facilities.

I want to start by talking about the Washington State Higher Education Coordinating Board. What is the mandate of the board? Overall, the mandate is to serve as an independent body that looks after the interests of higher education, apart from the interests of individual institutions. It consists of 10 members approved by the Governor and confirmed by the Senate. The board is also responsible for preparing a master plan for the state's higher education system, and we have been involved for 15 years or more in developing the branch campuses.

At the time you first started to think about this plan to co-locate a university branch campus and a community college, what would you say the board's biggest challenge was? Well, there were a number of different challenges and one was that we, in our master plan, had identified a need to serve an additional 60,000 students by the year 2010. We were trying to develop campuses in order to meet, in essence, the Baby Boom echo that the colleges were going to be faced with.

So our first priority was to create new campuses that would respond to the enrollment demand in the state, particularly in the urban areas. Back in 1987 we did studies on where new campuses should be sited, and the conclusion was, in western Washington, to have one in Vancouver, one in Tacoma, and one in the Bothell-Woodinville area. That was all related to population density, commute time, and projected growth.

These were the areas where it looked as though the population of people of college and university age was going to be occurring? Right.

You have to understand some background on this. The initial site for University of Washington Bothell was an area called Wellington Hills, but it was determined that that site couldn't be used even though it had been bought because it was outside the growth limit boundary.

At the same time we found out that the community colleges were seeking money to plan a new community college in that area, and one of the pieces of guidance we got from key state legislative members was that there was no way two campuses were going to be built within five miles of each other at the same time.

CHANGE TOOL IN ACTION: 08
DESIGN THE RELATIONSHIP

Initially, all the stakeholders in the Bothell project, particularly the institutions, saw co-location as an arranged marriage driven by the state legislature. There was no consensus on the value of the project and little trust in its success.

We began building trust by asking stakeholders a question about success: "It is as good as it gets when...?" Out of the answers they understood each other's hopes and fears. A common vision emerged about education, community and environmental and economic sustainability. Building on this, we began to "design" a new campus together. This process illustrated that there was no hidden agenda.

The relationships and the process became intertwined. The analytical rigor we went through ultimately turned antagonists into advocates. Content got us to common ground, got us approvals in half the normal time, and allowed us to meet the mandated campus opening date.

BILL SANFORD
Partner, NBBJ

There are obvious distinctions between a community college and a university—one grants diplomas, the other degrees. But beyond that, how would you describe the differences in terms of their approach to education and the people they serve? In the community colleges you have some people who aren't interested in a baccalaureate-level education. Some need basic education, some need technical training. But you do have those who want to get their first two years at a community college and then transfer to a four-year institution.

The big difference between a baccalaureate institution and a community college is that the community colleges have what's called an "Open Door Policy," and essentially anyone can attend a community college. The baccalaureate institution, and this includes University of Washington, has admission standards. This underlay a lot of the tension we went through trying to get the University of Washington to support the notion of co-location with a community college. They were initially reluctant to do that.

What kind of university is the University of Washington? It's a research institution, Carnegie Class One—like Berkeley or UCLA. It receives more grant money than any other research university in the country. It's major. There are 35,000 students. The main campus in Seattle is like a city in itself.

Were they responding to this idea of having to share a campus with someone else in much the same way that any university would? Yes. I went to different parts of the country and talked to people who had tried co-location. There's typically some resistance from the four-year institutions. It gets into values and institutional culture and things like that. The prior administration at the UW was opposed to the idea. The Board of Regents was opposed. But over time, I think once they started to see the potential of the campus, things turned around.

The other problem that we were addressing was the site itself. It has some significant environmental issues. That was a major challenge being addressed at the same time that we were trying to get the two institutions to be willing partners.

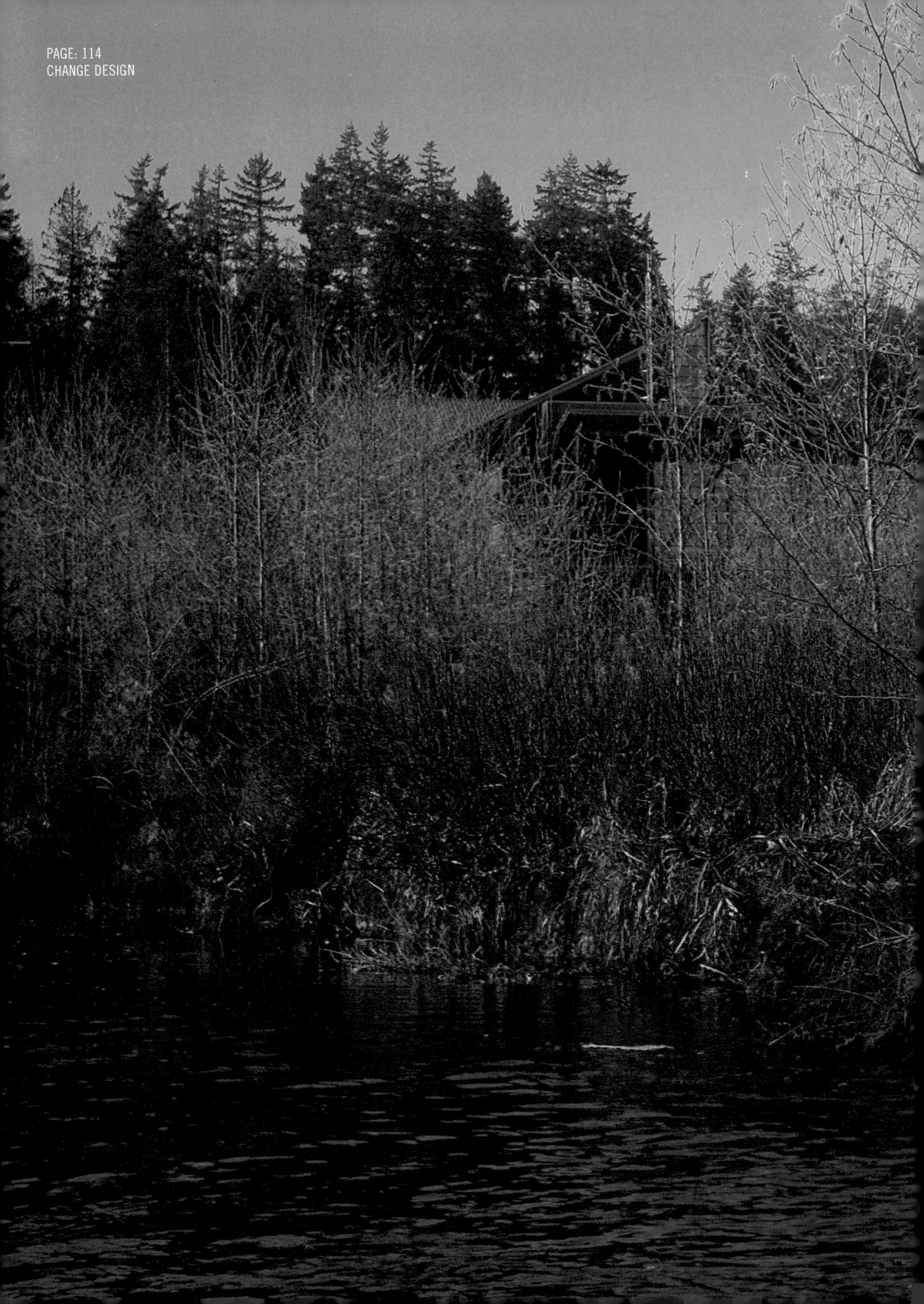

By regulation if the project was going to use the stream at all it had to be returned to being a salmon-bearing stream. And it was. You walk out on the boardwalk and see the salmon spawning.

THE GOAL OF THE PROJECT IS TO PROVIDE A QUALITY LEARNING ENVIRONMENT IN A MANNER THAT MAXIMIZES RESTORATION AND PROTECTION OF THE ENVIRONMENT.

Describe the site, and tell me a bit about why it was selected. It was selected because of its location. It's right off Highway 405. It's 130-some acres, but of that, about 55 acres are wetlands. We had to do a lot of analysis to make sure that the buildable area of the site could accommodate 10,000 students, because that was the build-out that we intended to have for the campus.

In this state, as in others, getting a permit to work on a wetland area is extremely difficult. It's administered by the Army Corps of Engineers. There was likelihood that we wouldn't get it from them. So we went through a number of activities to demonstrate to the Corps that technically and physically what we were going to do was worthwhile.

There was a creek that used to meander through the property years and years ago. It was moved to become a log flume.

This would have been, what, a century or so ago? Yes. Our plan was to move the creek back to its original area and then that would reduce the flooding that occurred on the site.

We eventually got the permit. A lot of that dealt with support from the community that had initially been opposed to the development of the site. Before we got involved with examining this site and potentially buying it, the owner had submitted plans to develop a regional shopping mall, and he was sued by the Washington Environmental Council, two other environmental groups, and the City of Bothell over his intent to fill the wetland.

When we got involved, that litigation was still underway. So we set up what was called a Site Development Advisory Committee and brought to the table the people who, a month before that, had literally been suing each other.

I also included representatives from the tribes and representatives from the Department of Ecology and Department of Transportation to work with us and develop a site plan that was acceptable to all the parties.

We'd meet monthly in the late afternoon or early evening down at NBBJ. We'd have a meal and sit and look at drawings and talk about concepts. The meal was important because, basically, if people will sit down and eat with each other, they're going to work out their problems. And they'd better have good food, too. There's a great Italian restaurant right behind NBBJ's building and they

THE RIDGE REVELATION

For about three or four years the design team was operating with an understanding that the site was an upper table and a lower shelf. The town of Bothell sat on the higher level, the freeway interchange was on the lower level, and the difference between the bottom and the top was a very distinct slope. Usually, steep slopes are the delicate and fragile parts of a landscape; you get erosion. So, generally, you don't touch the slopes. That's what was operating here.

All of the development options were occurring on the top level. The problem was that it displaced the conifers, a little remnant of forest that the community was very sensitive about. But if the development went below the slope, it would interrupt the restoration of a stream. So the design team was betwixt and between. Nothing worked up above, nothing worked down below, and the development options began to thin out until there was discouragement.

So NBBJ was withdrawn and another architectural firm began work on the project. They too zeroed out, because they too protected the slope. They went to the bottom land and displaced the wetlands. Within a year the project went back to NBBJ.

You can get fixed on an idea, and keep working on options for it. NBBJ had had 10 different campus plans for the upper level. And once you're that deep into an assumption it's hard to back up. Now, the abrupt changes of situation—another architect coming in, then receiving the project back—didn't feel good. But that's sometimes when freshness comes and the available answers start showing up.

And, indeed, that's when there was a revelation, this beautiful moment when the problem became the solution. The design team said, "What if this slope could be replaced? Put in a new slope, and let that be the campus. Protect the top, protect the bottom, and feed the

two institutions from end to end along the slope." Suddenly everything began to unfold. At one end of the slope was a smaller piece of property and at the other was a larger piece of property, so the University of Washington could take the heavy end and have its identity, and Cascadia, the smaller school, could take the smaller end and have its identity. We could save most of the conifers and restore the stream.

Most effective designers, whether architects or engineers or landscape architects, believe the same thing: if you are really creative with understanding the issues and the problems and the nature of a place, you will find the answer; it's usually inherent in the circumstances at hand. You don't have to invent the answer, you don't have to bring it in from Italy or somewhere else in the world; it's there. It's a question of uncovering it.

BILL JOHNSON
NBBJ

CHANGE TOOL IN ACTION: 12
BREAK BREAD

Once a month, NBBJ held a stake-holders meeting that ran through the evening. During these meetings there would be all this fighting, arguing, sometimes even yelling, and then people had to sit down and share a meal. It was like a family—there's an argument, but you sit down and eat dinner together.

LIZ JACKS
Principal, NBBJ

The value of breaking bread—coming together with food to discuss ongoing challenges—was a civilizing influence that changed the context for communication and created common ground. When the plan went through the final environmental review, when it went through the city process for approval, when it went through the federal process for approvals—approvals were gained in record time with very little formal opposition.

BILL SANFORD
Partner, NBBJ

would cater the meals. It was great. If you can get people to commune, then they don't fear each other.

And it worked. I can remember when Bill Sanford [of NBBJ] and I went to get the final permit approval from the City of Bothell, the hearing examiner—who's like an administrative judge overseeing testimony—stated at the end, when he presented his findings, that this was the first time he'd ever seen a project that had no opposition. When you think about that in the context of the magnitude of this project and the environmental issues that were present at the site, that was a pretty rewarding statement.

You think you were able to accomplish that because of this process that you went through? Oh, definitely.

We also did a lot of external things to demonstrate that the community was behind this. We held countless community forums in the area where people could come and see how the campus would look. Lots of media. We would routinely brief key legislators. We'd do that both in Olympia and up at the NBBJ [Seattle] office.

Clearly you were a champion of that. Why were you convinced it could be a good thing? It was going to have to be. Once we had had to rule out Wellington Hills because you couldn't build there, this site was it.

So you had to make lemonade out of lemons? Yes. We needed a campus up there. There are very few developable sites in the area. So it was imperative that we figure out a way to succeed in acquiring the property and developing it for the campus.

You had very few precedents to look at, correct? Had this not been done very successfully elsewhere in the country? No. Many, many potential projects don't go forward because people can't get the wetlands permit, and a key element of the project was restoring the wetlands. And nothing in the country had ever, and to this day has ever, been done of that magnitude. Typically a project might have half an acre of a wetland that you have to mitigate. In other words, if you build on that you've somehow got to go and acquire some other property to preserve the wetland. This was up to 60 acres.

So you had not one, but two precedent-setting opportunities, or challenges depending on which way you look at it: this very large wetland restoration, and the bringing together of a college and a university in a co-location. Yes. In fact when I wrote the project plan and put out the Request for Proposals, I had worked through in my mind what the goal of this project was, and it was two things, but I didn't want to separate them because I didn't want to get into, "Is the first one more important than the second?" So I wrote something to the effect that the goal of the project is to provide a quality learning environment in a manner that maximizes restoration and protection of the environment. Those aren't the exact words, but it was a way to recognize both things we were trying to do.

Let's get back to the point at which you had everything in place except for the agreement of the University of Washington. How did you ultimately get that? Well, there was a change in university administration, a new president, and I think that was instrumental. I think the public support was instrumental. And once the actual people who would be working at the campus were getting together and doing what's called the programming phase, then that really helped. Because they could see each other, and see that they weren't, you know, Martians.

What was NBBJ's role throughout this process? They were my right arm. They and their sub-consultants. They were planning in an architectural development sense, but they were also managing all these different forces with me.

It certainly sounds like a marshalling of forces was one of the real challenges here. Yes. We opened a storefront office in this little village of Bothell, and NBBJ would staff it four days a week, and we'd have drawings up and cookies, coffee, and invite people off the street in. We had a newsletter that went out quarterly, and it would talk about the project, where we were. We had a very long mailing list.

We had these external strategies and I think when the administration changed at the university and the actual faculty members sat down to do the programming of the spaces with the community college, I think that was key. It was getting to that point that was a little rocky at times. There were many times when this project could have died. Many times.

What was the history up to that point of the concept of co-located higher education institutions? Some had worked across the country, some had been dissolved, some were still operating but not very well, and there were a few success stories. One of the things we did to get ourselves educated, but also to help the UW to see that it wasn't going to hurt, was to hold a symposium. We brought in people—I believe it was from five different states, including Hawaii, Texas, Florida, and Kentucky—people who were at successful and unsuccessful co-location sites. It was a two- or three-day conference, and each of those parties got up and went over how they had approached co-location, what went well, and what failed.

What came out of that? Lessons learned. One that comes to mind immediately was the need for the two institutions to have a joint operating agreement that would clarify the respective roles and document their respective rights. That came from one of the states that made a presentation at our symposium. That was a key thing that the two institutions subsequently adopted, and it's still in force.

I can imagine that both institutions would have very much wanted to ensure that they had their own identity on this campus. Right. Every time we would meet with community members, we would make sure that the university and Cascadia people were there and we would always emphasize that this campus was going to preserve the identity and promote the identity of the two different institutions. We got that message out very clearly.

Long before the campus was built, when NBBJ prepared the renderings of what it would look like, it was a very student-oriented space. The circulation patterns through and around the buildings and how it would blend in with the hillside and the trees. I think when people started to look at what this place was going to look like, they said, "Hmm. That might not be too bad!"

According to an article I read about the opening of the co-located campus there was still talk that the differences between the university and the college—

*including funding, salary levels, and teaching loads—would be difficult,
if not impossible to surmount. What has happened since then?* I know people
were talking about that, but that differential is going to exist between any
community college and any four-year institution. That was my argument.
Those differences have nothing to do with co-location. Co-location doesn't
cause that.

Has being on the same campus started to subdue some of that sense of difference?
I believe so, yes. Norm Rose, University of Washington's dean, who's now retired,
he was pretty opposed to the co-location initially, and he hated the site. I remember after construction started, he called me one day and he said, "You know,
I've got to tell you, I had this whole thing wrong. I didn't understand the potential
that the wetlands restoration would provide to the students."

Because I had said, "Look, you're going to have the largest restored wetlands
in the country, and one program that's very big at the UW is Environmental
Sciences." When he saw that they could incorporate that resource, the wetlands,
into an academic program, he was excited.

*Can we talk a bit more about that? How is the campus, now that it's been open
for several years, serving the people that you initially set out to serve back in
the early '90s?* It's doing great. Both the institutions offer good programs. The
first phase, as students filled it up, has actually exceeded the enrollment plans.
The interest side is there. The demand to attend there exists. And the output is
there. They're graduating students with AA degrees and baccalaureate-level
degrees. And that's what we wanted.

*And what do you hear from the community that was initially so opposed to this
site being used?* Well, every member of the Advisory Group, at the final hearing—
when we had a final hearing on the Environmental Impact Statement—got up
and supported the project. Every single one. They said that it was a good thing
for the environment, that it was a good thing for the City of Bothell, and that
it was a good thing for the students.

THE GREAT OLD MAPLE

One of the factors in all of the plans that were made was this tree. It's a great old maple, and it stands on a little slope. There was a farmhouse, and the maple was in the front yard. And everybody would say, "There's no way we can keep that grand old tree because there's too much program to fit in there." So the secret little challenge for the design team was: we're going to save that tree, and it's going to become special.

When the project moved, finally, to the idea of the lineal campus, the tree became part of the retained space. And during the construction of the campus, as proof of the attractiveness of this one grand old tree that most people would have taken out years ago, the contractors, these tough guys in these big machines, would shut off their big machines and climb this dusty little hill, and they'd all gather under this maple and have their lunch. And on the day the campus opened, the first day of classes, there was an instructor talking to this class of about 40 guys and girls—all sitting under the maple tree.

BILL JOHNSON
NBBJ

AT THE FINAL HEARING THEY SAID THIS IS A GOOD THING FOR THE ENVIRONMENT, A GOOD THING FOR THE CITY, AND A GOOD THING FOR THE STUDENTS.

Do you get a sense of what it means for the students of both institutions to be sharing with each other? I think for the community college students, those who don't immediately have a plan to get a bachelor's degree, there are some who don't go further because they don't believe they'd be able to succeed. My theory was that they could see other people like themselves, enrolled as juniors at the University of Washington, succeeding, and just by association, by talking with them, be encouraged. I don't have any measure that that happened, but I think it did.

Since the national consensus initially was that a co-location of a community college and a university either shouldn't or couldn't be done, what kind of interest have you been fielding in the project? I think there have been three different doctoral students who did dissertations on it. All kinds of other articles have been written about it. It got a national award for planning from an international education planning group. There have been a lot of inquiries as to how it got done.

What do you tell people who call to inquire? People from other states who want to try to do this themselves? The key thing is to get the goal and stay focused on the goal, and keep that in front of you and all the people who you're going to have to work with. ✦

SAIL OF THE CENTURY

City Developments Limited, the Sail @ Marina Bay
residences, Singapore, Completion 2008.

The Singapore government wants Singapore to become a global city. It is already a gateway city. Within the radius of seven hours' flying time you have two billion people traveling.

KWEK LENG BENG
Executive Chairman,
City Developments Limited (CDL)

Singapore is in constant competition with Shanghai and Hong Kong and we, as architects, can help Singapore compete.

PETER PRAN
Principal, NBBJ

To survive in a competitive world, we need to be a few steps ahead. The business sector must take advantage of the government environment and achieve not only our own private vision but the vision of Singapore as a whole.

K.L.B.

en he first met us, Chairman Kwek
d us he wanted a building that
resents Singapore's future.

OTHY JOHNSON
ner, NBBJ

People love waterfronts, and Singapore is
the only major city in Southeast Asia that
has one. The government wanted to build
a new financial city facing the sea, like
Canary Wharf. We decided to pioneer residential living on Singapore's waterfront.

K.L.B.

Singapore's central business district has
been a 9 to 5 enclave. This is the first
housing project to be built there. This
will diversify activity and stretch the life
within this area to 24/7.

T.J.

When you arrive in a city your first impression is the skyline. You never forget your first look at New York's skyscrapers. I wanted something that any visitor coming to Singapore would remember Singapore by.

K.L.B.

We asked ourselves, "What's unique about Singapore as a place?" It's an island. Being on the water, the wind is always there. And it's nearly on the equator, so the sun is intense. Water, wind, and sun "shaped" the building.

T.J.

Most developers will not do this kind o' building because it costs 35 percent more than usual. I was prepared to spend 35 percent more because I belie' we can sell it better as an iconic building.

K.L.B.

they are well received, buildings create a cultural statement for a city. Early in the 20th century the Bauhaus movement thought architecture was the cure to all social ills. It may not be that, but it can transform a society.

Because our population is so small we need a lot of foreign talent living here to help Singapore grow faster. In the old days, the residential market had 20 percent foreign buyers, mainly from Asia. The Sail @ Marina Bay has slightly more than 40 percent foreign buyers, from as far away as the UK and the US.

It has changed Singapore to be more international in its development.

K.L.B.

JUSTICE SERVED

Seattle's US District Court made a federal case out of stage sets and sightlines, libraries and lily ponds in order to build a courthouse that inspires awe, comfort, and judicial efficiency.

U.S. DISTRICT COURT OFFICE OF THE CLERK

GENERAL INTAKE
FILE REQUESTS

CREATED AS THE OUTGROWTH OF THE HOOVER COMMISSION IN 1949, THE GENERAL SERVICE ADMINISTRATION (GSA) SECURES THE BUILDINGS, PRODUCTS, SERVICES, TECHNOLOGY, AND OTHER WORKPLACE ESSENTIALS THAT FEDERAL AGENCIES NEED.

THE GSA'S PUBLIC BUILDING SERVICE IS THE LARGEST COMMERCIAL REAL ESTATE ORGANIZATION IN THE UNITED STATES. IT PROVIDES 34.5 MILLION SQUARE FEET (3.2 MILLION SQUARE METERS) OF WORKSPACE FOR MORE THAN ONE MILLION FEDERAL EMPLOYEES IN 2,000 AMERICAN COMMUNITIES.

IN THE 1990S, THE GSA UNDERTOOK THE LARGEST COURTHOUSE CONSTRUCTION PROGRAM IN MORE THAN 50 YEARS. THE US COURTHOUSE IN DOWNTOWN SEATTLE IS ONE OF THE PROJECTS RECENTLY COMPLETED AS PART OF THE GSA'S DESIGN AND CONSTRUCTION EXCELLENCE PROGRAM. ACCOMMODATING 500 EMPLOYEES, IT TRIPLES THE SPACE OF THE COURTHOUSE IT REPLACES, WHICH WAS BUILT IN 1938.

THE NEW 23-STORY, 615,000-SQUARE-FOOT (57,135-SQUARE-METER) FEDERAL COURTHOUSE ENCOMPASSES A FULL CITY BLOCK IN DOWNTOWN SEATTLE. THE STRUCTURE HAS THREE PRIMARY COMPONENTS: A COURTROOM TOWER, JUDICIAL CHAMBERS, AND OFFICE BAR.

IT HOUSES THE US DISTRICT COURT, US BANKRUPTCY COURT, UNITED STATES ATTORNEY, AND OTHER COURT-RELATED AGENCIES.

IT INCLUDES 13 DISTRICT COURTROOMS, FIVE BANKRUPTCY COURTROOMS, AND 22 JUDICIAL CHAMBERS SUITES.

THE COURTHOUSE IS THE NATION'S FIRST TO INCLUDE UNIVERSALLY SIZED DISTRICT AND MAGISTRATE COURTROOMS, REDUCING THE NUMBER OF TOTAL COURTROOMS NEEDED. COURTROOMS AND JUDICIAL LIBRARIES ARE SHARED, WITH EACH COURTROOM FLOOR CONTAINING THREE JUDICIAL CHAMBERS ADJACENT TO TWO COURTROOMS.

BRUCE RIFKIN

DISTRICT COURT EXECUTIVE, UNITED STATES DISTRICT COURT, WESTERN DISTRICT OF WASHINGTON

For over 20 years, Bruce Rifkin has served as District Court Executive/Clerk of Court for the United States District Court for the Western District of Washington. He was appointed as Deputy Trial Court Administrator in Dade County Florida [Miami] and Attorney/Advisor for the Administrative Office of the United States Courts prior to moving to the Western District of Washington. He has held positions as chair of the Ninth Circuit Clerks Liaison Committee and national representative to the District Clerks Advisory Group. In 1998, he received the Directors Award for Outstanding Leadership, which is awarded nationally to one or two individuals in recognition of contributions to the federal judiciary. The award was given for the development of a comprehensive training program for federal judges and senior managers participating in the planning, design, and construction of new courthouses.

Let's start by talking about traditional federal courthouses as they were first built, 200 years ago, in cities across America. What were those buildings supposed to say to Americans? In the early days they were the center of the community, on the town square. They were often the most solemn, formal structure, and even as cities began to grow in the 18th, 19th, and early 20th centuries, they were often the most formidable structure in town.

"Formidable" implies something that people would approach with a certain amount of awe. Awe, and solemnity. The old courthouses mirrored classical architectural treatment; they had columns and details you didn't see in other buildings. From one town to the next, you could recognize the courthouse without having to read what was on the mantel because it was always the most prominent civic building.

And what was Seattle's old federal courthouse like? The tradition that I'm talking about started on the east coast. By contrast, we're a relatively new part of the country. Our old courthouse was constructed in the 1930s and, although people don't like to acknowledge this, it wasn't much of a building. It was part of the New Deal construction approach, where a government architect said, "This is what courthouses are going to look like: a rectangular box." The court-house in Los Angeles was built at the same time and it looks very similar, just larger.

How did it function for you, in your role as chief clerk? I'm in my 27th year here, and from my perspective, the old courthouse was not really very functional. Here's an example. Since the courthouse was first built, it's become increasingly, critically important to segregate judges and prisoners, for security reasons. In the old building there was no segregation. The prisoners went down the hallways, and even into the elevators, with the judges.

And it was not a very flexible structure with respect to 21st century technology. In the old days, at best you had a phone line. Now if you needed to cable the building it was a nightmare. It had cement floors two-and-a-half-foot thick. It also had large pillars that didn't make for an atmosphere very conducive to working.

As we've been discussing, some of these problems would have been the same in courthouses of the same age across the country. In the 1980s, the General Services Administration inaugurated a very ambitious program to build new courthouses. What was the goal of that federal program? The GSA is the developer for the federal government. Prior to the 1980s it hadn't built a new courthouse in something like 20 years. What happened during that time is the judiciary grew without gaining any additional facilities. You can't move a trial court. You can't move prisoners into a private office building. So the courthouse had to displace everybody that it could. By the time we had a new building, the bankruptcy court, the probation office, the pre-trial office, the United States Attorney were all in leased spaces.

At the same time, the GSA, through new leadership, created the program of design excellence. Our demand hit their program. One of the first courthouses that came to fruition was in Boston. The judges there wanted an extraordinary building to meet the judiciary's needs—and that's exactly what the GSA wanted through its design excellence program.

That program has since given the country many new courthouses that have become icons for the cities they're in. But one of the design precepts for the Seattle courthouse was that the icon element, design excellence, be balanced with functional performance. Why was the latter given equal importance in that equation? By the time we started to think about our new building, we could point to courthouses that had already been constructed—extraordinary icons, wonderful buildings—where a commitment to the excellence of what was inside, to the performance of the building, had, sometimes, been lost. I don't think it was lost out of ill will. It was because performance hadn't been made an absolutely committed goal of the architecture.

And we saw that. It's not a matter of being critical, but we would go into those buildings, on tours, and say, "My God, what an unbelievable piece of architecture, but man, it doesn't work!" At least in our view. And I haven't met a colleague yet who disagrees. There's always compromise, but it was our impression that functionality had not been given—I like the way you put it— equal importance.

CHANGE TOOL IN ACTION: 18
DESIGN THE PROCESS / JAZZ THE PROCESS

When we launched the project our team considered the delivery track record of similar federal projects. We realized that most ended in claims and litigation. Right then all of us—the judiciary, the GSA, and the design consultants— determined that we were going to write a different story. To do that we designed the process by which we would all collaborate before designing the project. We built deliberate activities into our game plan that would bring us together as a team, challenge our thinking, and allow us to discover ideas together, such as our touring activities and the effort to speak a common language. We defined our roles and set performance expectations together. We crafted a framework for decision-making from start to finish in order to realize design excellence while delivering the entire project on time and on budget. Along the way we actively cultivated understanding and built a team culture of empathy between the court, the GSA, the design team, and the builders.

STEVE McCONNELL
Partner, NBBJ

WE WANTED THIS TO BE AN INVITING BUILDING AND PLAZA, MORE INVITING THAN ANY OTHER SITE IN THE CITY.

At the same time that you had to balance iconic significance and functionality, within the functionality you had a balance as well. The building has to function for both the justice system and for the public. What was it that you wanted the building to say to and do for the American public? The challenge was to portray the importance and publicness of the building, without making it a fortress. That was the goal. I'll refer back to the old building. We had had the only lawn in down-town Seattle. We had green all around us, in a city that really doesn't have that. Now, we weren't going to put a lawn around the new courthouse—that doesn't make sense in the 21st century—but it was very important to have room on the site. That idea impacted the blocking of the building and led to us having towers.

When it came to the plaza itself, we didn't want it hardscaped. At a lot of the new courthouses, the plaza tends to be very hard. We didn't want ours to feel like a cement platform. So we have a forest of birch trees; we have pathways of stepping-stones with grass growing between.

We wanted this to be an inviting building and plaza, more inviting than any other site in the city. We wanted people from the neighborhood, people just walk-ing by, to come and sit.

So, really, quite the inverse of formidable. Yes. A place that is formal, but draws you in. And I do think it is both. The building has the formality; the plaza has the infor-mality. When you sit in the plaza you feel this extraordinary, strong structure around you, but you sit on benches, under the trees. Just today, we had music in the plaza at lunch, and people came to sit, to listen and eat. We have water features with lily ponds. We use them as a security device, to separate the secure area from the public area. That means when you come up the steps into the portico, you can actually go into the building without being immediately met by security. We have a strong and impressive building, but at the same time an inviting plaza and an open portico.

In terms of how the building needed to function for the justice system, you alluded a little earlier to how the federal court is home to many agencies. How do their needs differ? The hardest tenants are the judges, their courtrooms and chambers. Most of the other tenants primarily need office space. I don't want to diminish the other tenants' needs, but they weren't as difficult to address as the judges'.

Courthouses start with courtrooms. They're so complex that if you don't think through how you're going to meet those challenges, they may not work. So the goal was to try to create a kind of a tripartite building, where the first part was the courtrooms, the second was the judges' chambers adjacent to those courtrooms, and the third part was all the rest.

Early on, the judges were sent a questionnaire, as part of an effort called Enhanced Office Programming. What did it ask of you and your colleagues? There was a questionnaire and a set of interviews. NBBJ asked us to define what we do, how we operate, how we would like to operate. They asked us not to just accept what we did before as necessarily what we ought to be doing now. We were in a position to make changes if that would be beneficial. The process led to some very interesting changes from the way we had previously operated.

What changes were most significant? For the judges, I'll be specific. Each judge is entitled to a certain square footage that includes a reception area, a library, two offices — one for each of the law clerks — the judge's personal office, and a workroom/lunchroom combo.

When NBBJ did the Enhanced Office Programming, they asked about that configuration. What's good about it and what's bad? If you had the chance to change it, what would you do? What do you want from your space? And out of all that discussion a couple of things came out. One, with the advent of electronic access to law books the judges recognized that to build another library for each of them really didn't make any sense. The kinds of things that are not on-line tend to be specialty publications that certainly could be shared.

The other thing that came out of the discussion was this: our federal judges get the top law students in the world; they come in to work for law school credit. But you can't build space for these students because they're not in our design guide. The guide hasn't recognized that these people exist, yet they do. The answer can't just be, "Let's add to the square footage." You have to work within the space that's allowed.

We melded those two observations. One, that books are not so much less important, just less necessary, and two, that we need space for people who provide invaluable service to us but are not in the program. So, NBBJ came out from Enhanced Programming with a design that has three chambers on a floor sharing one central library. We reduced our collection of books by two-thirds—that's a huge savings in money. And the central library is a wonderful, two-story space with floor-to-ceiling glass and room for these beautiful carrels for the externs.

The plan was square-footage neutral but the judges ended up having space organized in a fashion that, if you walked through it with them, they would say they love. It gives them much more functionality than they had before, than they would have had if we had divided the space as authorized under the design guide. That was all a direct product of Enhanced Programming.

One other significant change involved my office, the clerk's office. In many courthouses, including ours, it's on the main floor. Usually, you walk into the grand public space, then go through a set of doors saying, "Clerk's Office" and end up in the transaction space—a big waiting area with a counter. I said, "I just don't like that." When I see a grand space, I want to interact with it directly. So, part of our design is that we have two grand spaces: a large portico and then a seven-story atrium. And my intake is part of that atrium. It goes to what I want the public to feel. I want them to realize that when they're thinking, "Oh, man, this is an extraordinary atrium, with a glass skylight seven stories up"—that extraordinary place is where they do their business.

When you were describing the outdoor public spaces, you talked a bit about security. Construction began pre-9/11, but the building was completed in the post-9/11 world, where security's even more of a major issue for everyone than it already was. We faced the security issues pre-9/11, but you're right, everyone is more conscious of it now. You know that we had somebody who tried to get in here with fake hand grenades, a couple of weeks ago [June 2005]; did you realize that?

THE GSA IS REDOING THE JUDICIARY DESIGN GUIDE AND CHOSE THIS BUILDING, OUT OF ALL OF THE FEDERAL COURTHOUSES, TO LOOK AT.

CHANGE TOOL IN ACTION: 10
INVEST IN TRAVEL

One thing about touring is that it's important to be focused, so the team identified sites ahead of time for particular reasons. One site was included for technology integration, another for aesthetics. The team targeted why they were going to a site, what they were looking at, and what they were looking to understand, so a lot was learned. Of course, touring with clients is one of the best ways to have the entire team focus, to learn a common language, and create a common reference. So the tour was an important building block in making a quality collaboration with the judges.

BILL BAIN
Partner, NBBJ

Yes, let's talk about that. There was a violent incident at the courthouse where an armed man was shot and killed inside the lobby by security guards. How did the building function during that emergency? The building as a building, as a design, functioned the way we would hope it would function. The man was contained in the front by security, and that's all we could ask for. That's what we did ask for. I guess we could have made it even harder for him if we had done what other courts did, which is to just put up a wall instead of using a water moat. And we will make some minimal changes to the water feature; we'll put in some wonderful architectural features so people can't shimmy along the little wall that we do have there. But I think everyone is quite satisfied that, even though we had the openness, it did provide the security. Any concerns we have post-incident have to do with our internal command and control. The building was fine.

You had a national workshop not long ago that brought judges from all over the country to Seattle, and they had an opportunity to see your new courthouse. What was the general response? A variety of groups have tracked through. In September [2004], right after we moved in, there was a national conference in Seattle of the United States District Court judges. Judges came from new and old courthouses all over the country, and we toured them through our building. I think it's a very handsome building, and they were struck by that. But—for me this is the most important—they looked at those choices that our judges made under the Enhanced Office Programming and said, "My God, that makes sense. What a functional place."

The GSA is redoing the judiciary's design guide right now, and this building was the one chosen, out of all of them, to look at, because although we designed it under the old design guide, we were the only place that could demonstrate how you can think through what you can do with space that might give you better solutions. NBBJ showed us better ways to use the space to meet our goals and objectives. And it is a beautiful building. We didn't sacrifice anything. ✦

OHN C. COUGHENOUR

IITED STATES DISTRICT JUDGE, WESTERN DISTRICT OF WASHINGTON

dge John C. Coughenour is the Chief lge of the Western District of Washington d is the past President of the Ninth cuit District Judges Association. He has ved as chair of the Ninth Circuit Jury tructions and the Intracircuit Assignment nmittees, and as chair of the Ninth

Circuit Gender Bias Task Force. Judge Coughenour was born in Pittsburg, Kansas, and graduated from Kansas State College of Pittsburg in 1963. He received his Juris Doctor degree from the University of Iowa in 1966, where he was Order of the Coif and a member of the Board of Editors of the Iowa

Law Review. He taught trial and appellate practice at the University of Washington School of Law from 1970 to 1973. Judge Coughenour was a partner at the Seattle law firm of Bogle and Gates when he was appointed to the United States District Court in 1981.

Most of us get our ideas about justice from Hollywood, where a trial seems satisfying if there's lots of grandstanding and arm-waving. In real life, how do you measure the success of a trial? I think the ultimate measure is whether I'm satisfied, at the conclusion of the trial, that the right thing was done, that the jury came to the right verdict, or if it's without a jury that I was able to see facts that made me confident that I could rule one way or another and not do a lot of mischief. A lot of times cases that get tried are tried because there are good arguments on both sides, and it's sometimes very difficult to cut through all of it and feel really comfortable that you've done the right thing.

If you think about it, some of the best final arguments you've seen in movies or on television are probably in the neighborhood of two to three minutes. The producer of a TV program or a movie can't afford to spend more time than that on one aspect of the story. Well, in the same case, if tried in a real courtroom, those arguments would take hours instead of minutes.

And that makes more demands on you and on the jury. Yes. Sometimes it causes the jury or the judge to lose interest — in the middle of the afternoon when it gets stuffy and late and everybody's tired and the lawyers are droning on about something nobody cares about. A lot of good trial lawyers say that after 20 minutes in an argument you're going to have to fight to keep the attention of the jury or the judge.

I teach a class in how to try lawsuits, and one of the things I draw analogies to is the making of a movie, the presentation of a play.

Courtrooms are sometimes referred to as theatrical spaces. Is that what you're alluding to? Yes, I am. A movie or a play or a trial. They're all exercises in communication.

Over the course of your career you've worked in courthouses across the country. What are some of the ways that the physical space of a courtroom can help or hinder that communication? The most important thing, in my mind, is that when somebody walks into a federal courtroom they should have an immediate impression, subconsciously if not consciously, that this is an important place, that something extraordinary is about to happen here, that this isn't just another meeting room.

WHEN YOU WALK INTO A FEDERAL COURTROOM YOU SHOULD HAVE AN IMMEDIATE IMPRESSION THAT SOMETHING EXTRAORDINARY IS GOING TO HAPPEN HERE.

In some of our county courthouses, particularly in metropolitan areas, the counties have been so besieged by budget problems that whenever they look for places to save money the courts end up with short shrift. And, as a consequence, in a lot of our county courts, the feeling you get when you walk into the courtroom is this is a scruffy, not very clean place where dirty business is done.

The federal courts, on the other hand, have been very successful in persuading Congress that it's extremely important that our courthouses and our courtrooms be a statement of federal presence in the community, and that when people walk into the courtroom they realize that this is a significant and very important place.

There are some classic examples around the country of courtrooms in older buildings that are ornate and exquisite places—carved walnut and marble and the like—but you just can't afford to do that sort of thing anymore. It's hard for architects now to design a courtroom that accomplishes everything that we want to accomplish. NBBJ spent a lot of time with us talking about these things.

Have the demands that the justice system places on a courtroom changed over the course of time? No, not really. Going back to the thought I mentioned earlier, it really is an exercise in communication and, by and large, we still try cases the way Abe Lincoln did, with a lawyer standing up in front of a jury or a judge and talking to them and communicating with them.

There are a few things that have changed—and for the better. Electronic document handling has sped up document-intensive cases, and the electronic document-handling system we have in this building is state-of-the-art; it helps us move trials along faster. Real-time court reporting is another example of something that is a little different since I started practicing. Now we get a transcript on the computer screen a few seconds after the actual words are spoken. And the ability of lawyers to access the Internet from counsel table in the courtroom and do legal research right from counsel table with their computers is something else that is different. We did some of that in our old building and it required jackhammering concrete floors to create tunnels for cable. This new building has a cable vault below the floor so that it's a lot easier to make modifications as technology changes.

The other thing that has been a significant improvement is the ability to put monitors in the jury box for the jurors to see documents up close. For example, if a witness is testifying about a particular document, and a lawyer is focusing the witness's attention on a particular sentence in the document, the document is on a monitor right in front of the jurors while it is also in front of the witness and the lawyer and the judge, and then the lawyer can highlight the sentence and the yellow highlight comes up on the monitor.

So the jury's focus is centered on what everybody's talking about, whereas before you either had to use an overhead projector, which was clumsy and often very difficult to locate in the courtroom so everybody could see it.

Another area where technology has been successful is sometimes we have to read testimony, from depositions or the like. The old approach was to have somebody on the witness stand who was reading the answers and the lawyer reads the questions and everybody goes to sleep.

Now, they do that but at the same time the transcript is scrolling down the screen on the monitors with a highlight that is following where the witness is in the reading, so that the jury and the judge and everybody else is on the same page, and it's a little more effective.

You mentioned that NBBJ spent a lot of time getting to know you and your needs. You, along with a number of your colleagues, were asked to fill out a questionnaire about those needs, and the design team responded to it by showing you images. They called it a "Visual Design Dialogue." What struck you as the most important questions and images about courtrooms? I was very impressed with that whole process. At first I thought that I had more important things to do, but as I watched the architects change their view of things based upon what we said to them, I realized that we were really having a significant impact on what the final product would be.

For example, a number of us emphasized that not just the courtroom itself but the courthouse too ought to have a feeling that this is not just another office building. This is a statement of federal presence in the community. And one of the architects laughingly said, "Be careful when you tell an architect to build a monument!"

THE VISUAL
DESIGN DIALOGUE

We put together a questionnaire and asked the federal judges to fill it out. In a way, that was presumptuous of us, but they were willing to engage the case for the questionnaire: you live in the written world, the world of precedents, so the design team is going to meet you in your world with words and thoughts. The team took the judges' responses and associated with those answers a range of visual imagery, creating what's called a "Visual Design Dialogue." This then became a bridge from the written world to the visual

world of design. On the strength of these images, the design team and the judges established a common ground and common reference points.

The questionnaire was intentionally provocative. One of the questions dealt with classicism in architecture. The design team quickly moved the judges from preconceived ideas about the building to thinking "it's the idea of a portico that matters, not that it has the right order of columns." The Visual Design Dialogue showed Dulles Airport

and its colonnade — its clear organization and the verticality of the front façade is evocative of the federal presence in Washington DC and yet it's a modern interpretation.

Throughout the judicial system there are many stories of architects and judges gone astray and yet here was a relationship built on the substance of content and on the sharing of ideas and thinking.

STEVE McCONNELL
Partner, NBBJ

But to a certain degree that's what we were saying, that this is a building that is being built for a hundred years and should have some classic grandeur about it. One of the judges who was in town for our recent committee meeting had never seen our building and she didn't know where the courthouse was, she just knew the general direction. She was staying at the Grand Hyatt and she said as she came down 7th Avenue and approached Stewart, she looked across the street and said to herself, "That's it." And that's exactly what we were trying to accomplish.

The design process ended up in a full-scale mock-up that you could walk around in. What was that experience like, and what did you learn from it? One of the biggest problems in designing courtrooms is always line of sight. Going back to my original concept that a trial is an exercise in communication, you have communication between lawyer and judge, you have communication between lawyer and witness, you have communication between witness and judge, communication between lawyer and jury, communication between witness and jury, and judge and jury, communication between jury and monitors. All of these lines of sight and communication are critical to a trial because the interplay between the judge and the lawyers is important, the interplay between the lawyers and the jury is important, the interplay between the witness and the lawyer, the witness and the jury, the witness and the judge are all important.

And you're talking about communication not just on a verbal level? Yes, exactly. The judge, the jury, the lawyers, everybody needs to watch the demeanor of the witness. For example, a major portion of credibility determination is based upon body language: does the witness appear to be nervous, is the witness sweating, is the witness stammering? All these things help one make a decision as to whether somebody's blowing smoke in your face or not.

And in a non-jury trial in particular you need a very effective line of sight between judge and lawyer, because that's a source of a tremendous amount of information that the judge uses to make a decision about the case. Well, you can't modify the courtroom every time you have a change in whether it's jury or non-jury, or you have a motion argument where there's not even a witness involved. All of this has to be anticipated in setting up the courtroom. And every judge has his or her own point of view of what's important in terms of setup. So we spent a lot of time in the mock-up talking about individual preferences. By the time the mock-up exercise was over we had what everybody was satisfied was going to be the final design.

And in the end what you got was very close to the mock-up? Yes, it was.

You also used the mock-up to look at the materials and finishes. Why was that something to test drive? I suppose I'm as much to blame for that as anybody, because one of the things that I always felt set our old courthouse apart from just another office building was the beautiful walnut-finish woodwork in the chambers and in the courtrooms. So from the very beginning I was harping on paying attention to the quality of the millwork. Part of that was because I had tried a long case over in Helena, Montana, in a courtroom in a courthouse that was built without a whole lot of judge input; it was just a GSA project that nobody paid a whole lot of attention to and the millwork in that thing was an abomination. It looked like plywood that had had stain slapped on it.

And if you're trying to communicate the gravity of this occasion... It's awfully hard to do in a place where the workmanship is as shoddy as it was in that building. And, you know, the finishing didn't turn out to be as much of a problem as I thought it would be. The GSA was in sync with what I was saying, and the architects were careful. This is an area where you don't have to spend a lot of extra money to get good quality stuff, you just have to pay attention to the specifications. I was delighted with the quality of the millwork and the finishing that was done.

At the start of this conversation you talked about measuring the success of a trial in terms of communication. How do you see the new courtrooms working in that regard? They work very well. There are a couple of fundamentals that are important in a courtroom. One is good lighting. The architects did a very good job of paying a lot of attention to the quality of the lighting. In other courtrooms I've been in around the country, and even in our old building, the light was not as good in some places as it was in other places; it was spotty. And I've been in new

CHANGE TOOL IN ACTION: 15
MODEL IT /
FULL-SCALE MOCK-UPS

Courtrooms are theatrical environments in the way the faces of witnesses — their stress, the beads of sweat — say something to the jury. When the design team built a full-size mock-up of the courtroom, they hired a stage crew who was knowledgeable about lighting and aesthetics, rather than a contractor to nail up a bunch of plywood. We created an environment that replicated the finished courtroom, but used creative stage-set technology which, as an added bonus, is actually very inexpensive. It served its purpose by engaging the judges, who made subtle adjustments to perfect the space.

JIM TULLY
Principal, NBBJ

courtrooms where you'll see people bringing in supplemental lights, desk lamps and the like, because the overhead lighting is not good, or it has glare. But the lighting in these rooms is very nice.

And a large amount of it is daylight. Why is that important? It makes a difference in terms of people getting tired. With all the visual demands that are placed upon jurors and judges, it's important to have natural light. We had plenty of natural light in the old building but here the architects did a nice job of positioning the windows. First of all, they're behind the jurors so that the jurors aren't looking into bright light; it comes over their shoulders into the courtroom. And secondly, the windows are high enough and the baffles are situated such that your attention isn't drawn outside, away from the courtroom, and yet you still have the natural light coming into the courtroom. In the old building you had to keep the drapes drawn to keep jurors from looking out at the trees or seeing whether it's raining. Here we don't have that problem.

The other thing that's extremely important in a courtroom is acoustics, again as a communication exercise, and the acoustics in the old building were not that good. We had terrible problems with the PA systems. They were antiquated, and the wiring was bad. The electronic communication system in this building is just superb.

Another thing that has surprised me a little was I had a big case, a criminal case, involving a total of about 12 defendants, and each of them had at least one lawyer, so you've got 24 to 30 defendants and lawyers, and then a team of lawyers for the government. Ideally the courtroom would have been half again as big as it was, but I was surprised at how well we were able to handle that many people.

In the old courtroom it would have been a real hassle. Here, the architects custom-built counsel tables that are units. You can add more units and not change the appearance of the tables.

Each of the things you're describing—each one on its own is a subtle thing, a small thing. And yet what you're describing is a place where every small thing that happens has an impact. Well, it should, if it's being done the way it's supposed to be done.

I can remember in college being told that one of the signature characteristics of Greek tragedy is that every word contributes to the central theme. That ought to be true of a trial if it's being well-tried. A tremendous amount of stuff happens in a very short period of time, stuff that somebody's going to be living with, in some cases, for decades, and so what happens there is extremely important. Whether you have a good view of the witness and can easily watch the witness's facial expressions and body language as the testimony's going on, and whether it's easy for the jury to move their focus from the witness to the lawyer. If it requires them to turn their entire body around they won't do it, and yet it's important for them to be able to watch both of these things easily, and that's hard to accomplish in most courtrooms. It's all a compromise, but you get it as good as you can. You can't get it perfect and accomplish all these things because some of them are exclusive to others.

But when you get a balance of those little things, justice works. Well, it works better. ✦

THE COURTHOUSE OUGHT TO HAVE
A FEELING THAT THIS IS NOT JUST
ANOTHER OFFICE BUILDING.
THIS IS A STATEMENT OF FEDERAL
PRESENCE IN THE COMMUNITY.

CHANGE DESIGN TALKING POINTS:
A BREATH OF FRESH AIR

Vulcan Real Estate's Alley 24 mixed-use project and new NBBJ headquarters, South Lake Union, Seattle, 2006.

We're a company that likes to be part of city building, and South Lake Union is the next expansion of downtown being done by the next generation of Seattle's founding fathers. A city dies if it doesn't change.

SCOTT WYATT
Partner, NBBJ

The neighborhood is 100 years old, and it has always been on the forefront of innovation. It had a Model T factory and Boeing built early seaplanes there. Now it's attracting what is known as the creative class.

ADA HEALEY
Vice President, Vulcan Real Estate

The building is addressing the creative class in a number of ways, from the tenant's perspective as well as an architect's perspective. It's about the quality of the workplace.

S.W.

product we're designing responds to ferent types of organizations, but the mary target users are early adopters, o see around corners and are open to ideas and new ways of doing things.

Since we're one of the first, we're thinking about the project as a prototype for a neighborhood fabric. We're creating well-scaled urban infill buildings with a strong overlay of sustainability.

BRENT ROGERS
Principal, NBBJ

To build a progressive building, you have to think out of the box, and to do that you have to be willing to take a little bit more risk than the average developer.

A.H.

When we look at projects, we're looking at achieving a "triple bottom line": generating a market return on our capital investments, making a positive impact on the community through quality design, and protecting the environment through sustainable development.

A.H.

Of course we want to build things that have a lower impact on the planet. But there is also a human side to sustainable design. It results in more natural light and more fresh air, and studies show that increases productivity.

S.W.

In a temperate climate, you can cool a building by opening the windows, so 40 percent of our windows are operabl You might say we're creating a buildin that breathes.

B.R.

BJ's decision to go into this building s based on the fact that we will have re ideas and get more work done. The I equation of cost per square foot per ployee is irrelevant. The new measure roductivity per square foot.

As the evidence in terms of productivity improvements becomes more widespread we think that every new building will adopt many of the features ours has.

A.H.

It's about providing a workplace where people want to come to work, enjoy being there, and can get their work done faster so they can go home and be with their families.

B.R.

NET WORKS

At the California Institute for Telecommunications
and Information Technology at UC San Diego,
Larry Smarr links scientists and artists in a
new kind of team building.

THE CALIFORNIA INSTITUTE FOR TELECOMMUNICATIONS AND INFORMATION TECHNOLOGY (CALIT2) IS ONE OF FOUR RESEARCH INSTITUTES LAUNCHED IN 2000 THROUGH THE CALIFORNIA INSTITUTES FOR SCIENCE AND INNOVATION INITIATIVE.

CALIT2 FOCUSES ITS WORK IN THE CONTEXT OF TELECOMMUNICATIONS AND INFORMATION TECHNOLOGY AS THEY RELATE TO THE EVOLVING INTERNET. THE INSTITUTE IS CONDUCTING RESEARCH IN NANOTECHNOLOGY, LIFE SCIENCES, INFORMATION TECHNOLOGY, AND TELECOMMUNICATIONS (WIRELESS AND OPTICAL).

CALIT2 COMMISSIONED TWO BUILDINGS AT UC SAN DIEGO AND UC IRVINE TO REALIZE ITS TECHNOLOGICAL AND SOCIAL GOALS. FUNDING FOR THE CALIT2 BUILDINGS CAME FROM CALIFORNIA TAXPAYERS AS PART OF THE STATE'S $100 MILLION STARTUP INVESTMENT IN THE INSTITUTE AND WAS CONDITIONED ON CALIT2 RAISING AT LEAST TWICE AS MUCH FROM OTHER SOURCES.

SINCE DECEMBER 2000, CALIT2 FACULTY MEMBERS HAVE RECEIVED MORE THAN $226 MILLION IN FEDERAL RESEARCH AWARDS. INDUSTRY AND RESEARCH DONATIONS TOTAL APPROXIMATELY $78 MILLION TO DATE.

CALIT2 CONSTITUTES ONE OF THE LARGEST MULTIDISCIPLINARY RESEARCH CENTERS IN THE NATION. AT PEAK CAPACITY, THE NEW RESEARCH BUILDING, ATKINSON HALL, AT UCSD, WILL HOUSE 900 RESEARCHERS AND STAFF, MOST OF THEM WORKING ON PROJECTS LED BY FACULTY FROM MORE THAN 20 CAMPUS DEPARTMENTS.

THE RESEARCH PROJECTS UNDER CALIT2'S AEGIS BRING TOGETHER EXPERTS WHO TYPICALLY WOULD NOT BE HOUSED UNDER THE SAME ROOF, MUCH LESS IN ADJACENT LABS.

THE SIX-STORY BUILDING INCLUDES THE MOST ADVANCED CLEAN ROOMS IN THE NATION, MEMS LABS, IMMERSIVE VIRTUAL REALITY FACILITIES, AND A DIGITAL CINEMA THEATER.

LABORATORY SPACE IS SHARED SO THAT MULTIPLE INVESTIGATORS CAN MAKE USE OF A WIDE ARRAY OF SPECIALIZED EQUIPMENT.

LARRY SMARR
DIRECTOR, CALIFORNIA INSTITUTE FOR TELECOMMUNICATIONS AND INFORMATION TECHNOLOGY

Larry Smarr is the founding director of Calit2 and the Harry E. Gruber professor in the Jacobs School's Department of Computer Science and Engineering at UCSD. Smarr is Principal Investigator on the National Science Foundation (NSF) OptIPuter LambdaGrid project and is Co-PI on the NSF LOOKING ocean observatory prototype.

As founding director of the National Center for Supercomputing Applications (1985) and the National Computational Science Alliance (1997), Smarr has driven major contributions to the development of the national information infrastructure: the Internet, the Web, the emerging Grid, collaboratories, and scientific visualization.

He was a member of the President's Information Technology Advisory Committee and serves on the Advisory Committee to the Director of the National Institutes of Health and the NASA Advisory Council.

The State of California launched an initiative in 2000 to ensure that it stayed at the forefront of technological innovation. This was one of the sparks that led to the creation of Calit2. Why was the university drawn to this initiative?
The University of California is, in a sense, more like 10 universities than one university. If all 10 campuses worked together there'd really be no other university in the world that could compete. But, in fact, the 10 are isolated from each other, intellectually as well as physically. Many of them—Berkeley, UCLA, San Diego— are world class; however, they became world class by hiring individual faculty, and basing promotion around individuals. If you want your papers counted they'd better be single-author.

On the other hand, the problems that California faces are systemic problems— transportation, the environment, earthquakes, and so forth. These aren't like single-author papers. The University of California realized that if it could come up with a persistent horizontal collaborative framework that could pull together researchers from different disciplines and attack larger-scale problems, ones that would involve industry, or would be actualized out in the community, then they would get much more productivity out of their investment in buildings and faculty.

They envisioned four institutes that would be collaborative by nature. They wouldn't just build a building and bring in a bunch of superstars and let them do their own thing. Instead, it was a social engineering experiment. Each institute was focused on an area that was very fast-changing: QB3 is focused on quantitative biology; CNSI on nanosystems, and ours, Calit2, is focused on the future of the Internet. To a large extent, California's economy depends on that.

We received $100 million to build two buildings and 70 percent of that was going to the building here at the University of California, San Diego [UCSD]. The challenge was to put a persistent collaborative framework into architecture.

The formal mission of the institute is to extend the reach of the Internet throughout the physical world. That's a big mission. What did you figure it would take to accomplish this? We knew we needed more than people working on just bits and bytes. We needed the end user communities that were going to be transformed by the future of the Internet—people in electrical engineering, the environment, transportation, biomedical research, digital cinema, and networked computer games.

CHANGE TOOL IN ACTION: 14
GIVE CLIENTS THE KEYS
Any environment designed to integrate and develop the highest technology, whether it's a medical, research, or educational facility, will change—repeatedly—and fast. Calit2's focus is on the future of the Internet. They recognize that this requires diverse, integrated intelligence. Mirroring their vision of a persistent collaborative framework, we invited the client in as a co-designer. Sitting side by side from the beginning, we developed performance criteria for the building systems that would enable rapid change and a series of alternative concepts for how those systems could be realized. This was an important first step because we collectively realized that these systems would drive the cost of the building now and into the future. We immediately understood the price tag for different levels of flexibility and could assess value to refine and further develop concepts. By doing this together, we avoided the typical iterative, non-value-added process where experts present ideas to the client. It's easier to make tough, informed choices when you're in the driver's seat.

BRAD LEATHLEY
Principal, NBBJ

THE CHALLENGE WAS, HOW DO WE PUT INTO ARCHITECTURE A PERSISTENT COLLABORATIVE FRAMEWORK?

We decided that we would focus on integrating the component parts that the individual faculties and their students represent into working, large-scale systems of the future.

I invented what I called "living laboratories of the future." Now, you might think, "How can you invent the future, because if you've invented it, isn't it already part of the present?" For instance, your PC now is a gigahertz PC. I had my first gigahertz computer in 1988 and it cost $15 million. It took from 1988 until about 2003 for the cost of multi-gigahertz computers to come down to mass market affordability. We can build living laboratories of the future on technologies that are at the top of their cost curve and are coming down.

So when you're talking about the future you're talking about what the average person would perceive as futuristic. Exactly, because that's how people see it. The Internet started in '72. The protocols were written in 1990, 15 years ago. And yet you ask anybody, "When did the Web start?" and they say, "Oh, it's been great the last five years," because that's people's perception. When a technology has exponential growth it crosses the threshold of public perception and people finally notice it.

So, the question was, how could we build a building that would do three things: provide an internal and external architecture that would signify the future; encourage collaboration between people who are, in the rest of their professional lives, in an architectural environment that fosters individual work; and create laboratories and facilities that would be unique not only on our campus but on many campuses.

So when NBBJ said, "What exactly do you want in this building?" I said, "I want it to be an enchanted castle."

An enchanted castle? Think about all the Walt Disney movies you've seen with enchanted castles. What makes them odd is that inanimate objects talk to you. They're not alive, but you're in a world that is active, in which data is everywhere.

In our case, we want to do teamwork, but a lot of the team members aren't here in California. Instead of having a whiteboard on one wall in a room, you have 50-inch plasma panels. It's not a TV, it's a window, to your office, or the office of a colleague in Singapore, Toronto, or Amsterdam. It doesn't matter where, because

with worldwide fiber optics and high-definition video you have tele-presence. Instead of looking out your window and seeing what is physically several feet on the other side of the window, you can see anywhere in the world.

How did you get from the castle metaphor to the building you now have? Through many discussions with NBBJ and the faculty that would be in it. Two dozen departments have faculty in the building. We had artists, chemists, engineers, medical doctors sitting around talking about the layout and shape of the building. One of the amazing things is that NBBJ tore up and redid the entire volumetric layout of the building at least three times, because they kept seeing new pieces. We would say we had to have a state-of-the-art digital theater, we had to have a set of nanotechnology clean rooms, we had to have circuit labs and radio labs and photonics labs, and we had to have performance art spaces. And they would say, "Okay. This is really great! We've never put all these functions into any one building. In fact, nobody has ever done that."

And you're making the future. Yes. So what is it about the future that would tell an architect something? Namely, that they can't possibly know what we're going to be working on five or 10 years from now, and the building's going to be around for probably 50 or 100 years, so flexibility was the most important thing. We had to have it so that when you looked at a laboratory you couldn't tell what it was for, because if you could it was too specific, and might be obsolete.

And you also have a situation where the actual population of the building is changing all the time, as well? Yes. The UCSD building will house about 900 people. At least three-quarters of them are students, so they're constantly turning over. The space is allocated based on projects and there are about 50 projects at any one time. When your projects are done, you're gone.

And then...? Maybe you've got a new project.

But it'll be an entirely different use of the space, either by you or by another group. That's right.

LABORATORY DRAMA

In designing research buildings, the number one guideline is don't preclude the opportunity to conduct the research, and number two is find ways of building in a robust system for exploring the opportunities and enhancing the communication of people who are there. That's why on this project—really on any project—we work with people who create the future—from the beginning—as a team. We're constantly developing and testing and doing a lot of scenario planning—what would happen if they wanted to do this, and what would happen if they wanted to do that. It's a very iterative process where you test and redraw and test and manipulate and tweak and go back and forth, and eventually, together, you get to the point where the design's ready to be built.

There was a long list of consultants on this project, including people who you wouldn't normally pull into an architectural team for a research building, such as acousticians, and data and media experts who do sound reinforcement and design projection and sound systems. We also brought in theater consultants. The team came up with three major media spaces. There's the 150-seat theater, which will work in at least six configurations, from a formal musical theater to a digital cinema. The multi-use room has modular seating risers that can be arranged any way you want. And the black box is… I guess the best way to conceive of it is like the holo-deck in Star Trek—it's a virtual reality chamber.

BRAD LEATHLEY
Principal, NBBJ

You've been referring to performance spaces as though there was nothing unusual about having them in a science building, but in fact, putting artists and scientists next to each other in the same space is not the way things are typically done. Why was that important to your mission? I've always worked with digital artists, even though I'm a computer scientist and physicist myself. Society has artists for a lot of reasons, but one reason is that they're like the canary in the coal mine. They detect the future first. And anything that will help us understand earlier where the future is coming from is to our advantage. Another reason is that the technology we're working with is socially disruptive. You could argue that the fall of the Soviet Union would, to a large extent, have been impossible without the Internet and fax machines. In the United States, we're concerned about the permissible limits of the use of our ubiquitous sensor technology. How does society form laws and regulations and customs in an entirely new space in which privacy is an obsolete notion? Artists deal with all of this stuff.

So you're working not just with the technology but with the implications of the possible uses of the technology. Very much. That is, in some ways, the most important part of the future. Look at what Napster did to disrupt the record industry.

However, I'm the first high scientist on this campus who has ever paid any attention — much less given any resources — to the digital artists. The University of California's Center for Research Computing in the Arts is one of the two most long-

lived digital arts groups of any university in the United States. It's been going for
30 years. These guys were used to living underground, because nobody cared
about them, and I come in and put $10 to $15 million worth of the best facilities in
the country in their hands. This building has tremendous visual art capabilities.
We have digital spatialized audio labs, motion capture labs that the dance instruc-
tors use, a black box theater, a digital theater lab, and a giant virtual reality room.
Sony is putting the first of its high-resolution digital cinema projectors in the
United States in our building. Who's going to make the content? Not the engineers.
It would be really boring in that theater if it was solely a bunch of engineers.

Of course there's this incredible clash between the artists' culture and the science
and engineering culture. But, amazingly, when you talk to our artists and ask,
"What are you into?" They say, "Well, these guys here on the same floor showed us
what they could do with microscopes, so we're thinking a lot about nanoart." This
is the kind of crazy mixing that we wanted to happen and that the architecture
lets happen.

You're describing how the artists are being inspired by things they've seen in the
scientific labs. Are you seeing a flow in the other direction, back to the scientists?
Very much so. What the scientists need from the artists is new visual metaphors.
Let's say the scientists are trying to represent network traffic. Do you represent it
physically where the fiber cables are, or do you represent it abstractly in some sort

CHANGE TOOL IN ACTION: 01
CHALLENGE ASSUMPTIONS

From the start, this was supposed to be a very technical-looking building. The original idea was to have a metal panel system that would express the desire for a very high-tech, modern look, while being very economical and reliable. The difficulty was that a metal exterior cladding system would shut down the radio signals coming through all of the building's wireless locations. We challenged the idea of a metal system being the only or best way to express their goal of a technological expression by doing further research. We found a panel system which is a wood fiber-based plastic. It looks very high-tech, but it's transparent to radio frequencies. So, as far as expressing technology, the big opaque exterior walls are actually the most transparent, and the glass walls with aluminum mullions are the least transparent. This contradiction of the initial assumptions took a little getting used to.

FRED POWELL
Senior Associate, NBBJ

of communications space? There is no physical object that is network traffic, so there's no preconceived visual notion of what it would look like. The artists become part of these teams. They do some really interesting visual thing with the data. They're innovating in the abstract space of representation. Over the years, I have found this to be invaluable to the scientist.

This has been done before but not in a way that has been planned for, which is what you've done here with the institute. Yes. I took everything I've learned over the years and tried to take it from being an odd thing that had happened to something that the architecture would make more common.

The New York Times calls what you've created a "collaboratory." As far as I know, that term was coined about 10 to 15 years ago by Bill Wulf, who's currently the president of the National Academy of Engineering in the US. He was in charge of the computer science division of the National Science Foundation when he came up with the term.

There have been very few examples of collaboratories. What you're trying to build is an environment in which people can easily work together regardless of where they are in physical space. That means not just that you can see each other's PowerPoints, but that you can visualize any digital material on the fly.

Say you're working on environmental sensor nets and you've got photos coming in from a wetland. The fundamental things that you're sensing are humidity and wind velocity and salinity. How do you turn those back into a visual representation that can be shared over the network with biologists, chemists, and the people who built the network? You may have to bring in satellite imagery and overlay that with actual sensor feeds and so on. The whole Calit2 building is set up to enable that.

You're talking about creating a network that is extending well beyond the walls of the building itself. Very much so. That's why many of the living laboratories of the future are built in the community. For instance, we've been funded by the National Science Foundation to work with the first-responder community—the police and fire and emergency—to build an instrumented gas-lamp district. The gas-lamp quarter is a famous tourist attraction in San Diego and it tends to hold large events in which there are 50,000 people milling around. Occasionally there are fights and disruptions that could hurt a lot of people if the first-responders don't know about them early, so we're working with the city to evaluate which of the various technologies you could put there both to aid the first-responders and support citizens' right to privacy.

We'll be in the gas-lamp district shimmying up light poles, putting up technology that was developed in our building. Parts of our building are set up as advanced versions of this technology. They test the software integration and ensure that the technology is going to work if it gets rained on. The fiddling around and vetting part goes on in the building, but the deployment part of our living labs tends to be out in the community.

Was WiFi connectivity an important factor for the building because of this kind of work with the outside world? The entire building has high-bandwidth wireless and it isn't just for PCs or PDAs. We want to be able to put a temperature, humidity, or light sensor anywhere, and these come with miniature WiFi antennae. WiFi is still pretty low bandwidth compared to current gigabit Ethernet. We also have 1.8 million feet of gigabit Ethernet cable in the building, enough for 9,000 gigabit Ethernet drops—10 gigabit drops per person.

How did the design of the building morph in order to accommodate these needs? We had to look at the wireless transparency of the building. We evaluated materials for the ducts, the walls, and the facade depending on their transparency in the gigahertz radio band. Normally, you don't think about the electromagnetic environment of a building, or about how metal interferes with it being a conductor. There's something called a Faraday cage, which is made of wire mesh. Electromagnetic waves don't propagate inside of that cage. What we wanted was an "anti-Faraday cage." We wanted to have signals propagating throughout the building. The architects spent a lot of time on the way the building's interior steel frame was laid out and we chose Trespa, a composite material, for the exterior to minimize the blocking of electromagnetic waves.

The other thing about the interior is that there are no drop ceilings. When you look up you see the steam pipes, water pipes, and Ethernet trays. There were a couple of reasons we did that. One was the ease of access, but another was so that when people look around the building they see infrastructure. Imagine if your skin was transparent and you could see the infrastructure of your circulatory, nervous, and digestive systems. Right now we look like black boxes, so people don't think about the intricate systems inside us. Since we're about the future of information infrastructure, I wanted people to see the infrastructure, the bare bones and circulatory system of the building itself, so that they would think about infrastructure on a daily basis.

I've heard the building referred to as rough around the edges by design. Is that what you're getting at? Yes. On the one hand, when people look at the building from the outside, they think it's very futuristic. But when they're inside, they see all of this infrastructure and they sometimes say, "Why didn't they finish that off so it looks nice?" and I say, "Because we are information infrastructure engineers. Infrastructure is us. We think infrastructure's interesting so we don't want to hide it."

You want to be able to see how everything works. And how intricate it is. Everything about human society these days, at least in the developed world, is devoted to hiding all the little things that make the world work. I sometimes think if it wasn't for the people who actually service the infrastructure, we'd all be doomed. We'd never know how to fix anything. Our whole world is held together by infrastructure, and we want our students to think infrastructure when they go out in the world.

You talked earlier about the institute as a social engineering experiment. If it's an experiment, what's your hypothesis? My sense is that the natural state of the world is for people to work in teams of different specialties. But for the past hundred years the university has gone down this path of extreme reductionism in which they break everything down into the tiniest little components and then you're a specialist in that. I like to say that we put the "uni" back in "university."

When Bob Dynes, the president of the University of California, came to the dedication of Calit2, he said that these institutes are the future of universities, and that Calit2 is at the point of the spear, because it is able to naturally form and

I WANTED PEOPLE TO SEE THE INFRASTRUCTURE, THE BARE BONES AND CIRCULATORY SYSTEM OF THE BUILDING ITSELF, SO THAT THEY WOULD THINK ABOUT INFRASTRUCTURE ON A DAILY BASIS.

I STOP PEOPLE IN THE HALL AND SAY, "HOW'S IT GOING?" AND THEY SAY, "IT'S JUST SO FREE. YOU CAN THINK AND INVENT."

un-form, in an effervescent fashion over time, self-selecting teams to attack major problems. If universities learn how to do that, they're going to be incredibly valuable to society. And our students will come out assuming that's the way the world works. So they are our chief social engineering export. We want them to spread the disease.

We developed a layer-cake diagram for the building. We invented it because people said, "You're all over the map. How do you add up to anything coherent?" I said, "At the base level we're talking about new materials and new devices, the very tiny things that form the insides of everything—cellphones, sensors, the electrical systems in cars, the insides of televisions and radios. Then the next level up is the wireless and the optical networking that ties those things together with the Internet. The next layer above that are the different embedded software systems in your processors, cellphone, operating system on your PC, and so forth that make the Internet run. The top layer is the social transformations driven by the underlying technologies. What are the social, regulatory, and ethical evolutions that occur?

And just to clarify the layers, you're talking about conceptual, organizational, and even physical layers. As I talked to NBBJ about this they said, "Well, won't the networking guys just stay in their own layer? How will you get them to go vertically to talk to the environment people?" The diagram is stratified horizontally and the layers are floors. The living labs form these vertical conductive currents. In other words, if you're going to build an intelligent transportation test bed out in the freeways, you're going to need software people, networking people, and device people. These projects will create vertical currents that will automatically and naturally mix. They'll go in and select out of the layers the people they need, and they'll start having team meetings, and those team meetings will be vertical.

NBBJ translated that idea into the very architecture of the building, so if you look at it from the outside you'll see vertical rectangular forms that slide across floors in different ways. When I asked NBBJ what they were, they said, "Those are your vertical convective currents that are connecting the layers."

It sounds like the project to design the building was a collaboratory. Absolutely. That was critical to the successful outcome. The design of the building itself was the most important formative aspect of creating Calit2 as it exists today, because it

forced people at an early stage to come together from all these different disciplines, respect and listen to each other's opinion, and collectively make decisions. It formed our cultural DNA.

And set the conditions for what you were going to be doing once the physical structure existed. It built a lot of the early culture. You look at this building and then you go around and look at the other university buildings and you say, "Wow, how come these other buildings look so shabby by comparison?" It's because they have no freedom to innovate. In this building, I stop people in the hall and ask, "How's it going?" and they say, "Oh, it's so great to be here working at Calit2." When I ask, "Why?" they answer, "It's just so free, you can think and invent and make things happen. It's not clamped-down and bureaucratic the way the rest of the university is." ✦

CHANGE TOOLS

help clients use design to encourage and accomplish change, BJ has developed and adopted certain methods, or tools, that not part of the traditional design tool box. NBBJ has discov- d that by using these "change tools" in concert with the sign tools it is possible to design buildings that transform the y enterprises of all sorts work. This section of the book col- ts together the Change Tools used on the projects docu- nted in the Change Design Conversations.

tools are organized here into four categories: **Vision** tools p determine the right thing to do; **Collaboration** tools build nmon ground, enabling people to better work together;

Communication tools aid in establishing a shared understand- ing; and **Delivery** tools enable people to realize their vision.

Within those categories, each of the individual tools has a specific goal; it also acts as a framework to be customized for the client and the circumstance. To see how that works, flip back to the page mentioned at the bottom of each tool descrip- tion and read the anecdote by an NBBJ designer about the tool in action. The anecdotes demonstrate how Change Tools enable design teams to address issues of change across multiple dimensions: behavioral, relational, organizational, and perform- ance related.

CATEGORY: VISION

CHALLENGE ASSUMPTIONS

GOAL: GAINING NEW INSIGHTS AND DISCARDING TIRED CONVENTIONS.

SEE THIS TOOL IN ACTION:
PAGE 180

Be six years old again. Ask "Why?" until you're satisfied.

Ask obvious questions, even questions that might seem dumb, like "Why are we doing this?" "Why do it this way?" "What is this space for and why?" Then discard conventional answers. Free from the restraints of old definitions, you're open to do what hasn't been done before.

Assumptions can be deadly in any business. It's difficult to look past long-held success to see something truly new, but asking first questions again is essential for everyone — especially experts.

The best way to elicit new definitions is to create a trust-based environment. If "Can we look at this another way?" is treated as a useless question, the process has been hobbled.

Information is power. Overly broad or familiar definitions limit the information you can access. In order to make an organization different and stronger, you first must be able to see it differently.

CATEGORY: VISION

LET VISION DRIVE THE PROGRAMMING

GOAL: TYING NEED TO VISION.

SEE THIS TOOL IN ACTION:
PAGES 31, 62

Put the spreadsheets away for a minute and ask, "What is it we really want to accomplish? Not just now, but far from now."

Go beyond what you think the project limits are. "Programming"—the first phase of designing a building—identifies space requirements, develops critical functional adjacencies, tests layouts and "process flow" alternatives. Programming typically makes the building's first use the highest priority. Since companies change faster than ever, first use can equal obsolescence at move-in.

Programming can be used for more than measuring projected headcount and cataloging equipment, technology, and space needs. "Enhanced programming" helps get to the heart of a company's vision and operations by assessing behavior, work patterns, future goals and trends alongside practical space needs. In this way, program goals tie needs to the vision, targeting proactive change and capturing performance metrics across organizational and environmental measures.

Expand the boundaries of the challenge. Make the problem bigger than you initially think it is and you'll solve the root cause instead of simply addressing the symptom.

CATEGORY: VISION

KEEP YOUR EYES ON THE PRIZE

GOAL: INCORPORATING THE VISION EVERY STEP OF THE WAY.

SEE THIS TOOL IN ACTION:
PAGES 4, 96

Look up from the dailies. Focus on the big picture.

Find a way, any way that works, to remind yourself why you're doing a project and who's going to benefit.

Tying the built environment to your vision makes it a strategic asset rather than merely a commodity. In the drive to get things done, vision can get lost. Constantly and consciously keep vision at the forefront by integrating it into the rhythm of a project. Integrate the vision as a header into meeting notes as a regular reminder of where you're heading and why. The essence of the vision should be ever present in the team space, both physically and virtually. Given the duration of major projects, we all benefit from keeping the vision constantly in sight.

CATEGORY: VISION / COMMUNICATION

SITE SEE

GOAL: BROADEN YOUR VISION.

SEE THIS TOOL IN ACTION:
PAGES 41, 92, 117

Step outside. Look past your immediate boundaries to see what's possible.

Go beyond the organization to make critical observations about your place at all scales—the immediate site, neighborhood, city, state, country, world. Uncover potential opportunities, identify constraints, and unearth secrets. Look at how and where people move and gather. Look at streets, dynamic densities, defined spaces, diversity, history, compactness, or distinctive character.

Big ideas come from big picture viewpoints, and from the small things as well. Search for the unique physical and experiential characteristics of a site. This contextual thinking will contribute to better environments for people.

By cataloging and connecting diverse site influences, site seeing is a tool that provokes visionary thinking. Inspiration from these observations can transform a location into a special place by adding content, meaning, and values.

CATEGORY: VISION / COMMUNICATION

SIMPLIFY COMPLEXITY

GOAL: ESTABLISHING SYSTEMS THAT BRING ORDER TO CHAOS.

SEE THIS TOOL IN ACTION:
PAGE 15

Search for patterns and be ready to recognize them. They will simplify your life and your work.

Copernicus, Newton, and Darwin found patterns in the world that accelerated discovery. Complex, multifaceted situations can often seem chaotic and contradictory. Pattern recognition opens a direct route to simplicity and solution, releasing capacity that would otherwise be tied up in pursuit of needless complication. Actively pursue the moments when patterns materialize.

Think of patterns as catalysts for understanding systems. Recognizing patterns of use, flow, and change, all functioning at multiple scales, helps us to clarify our place in the world as individuals and, as an organization, to develop an appropriate and useful response. Long-range forecasting is one such method by which an organization's recognition of patterns is used to plot strategy and action.

By recognizing patterns of use, you can discover what is relatively permanent (long cycles of change) and what is adaptable (short cycles of change). This helps to determine long-term investment and short-term placement of expensive building infrastructure. In turn, you can identify elements that need the highest level of detail and how they might relate to a unified whole.

CATEGORY: VISION / DELIVERY

WORK WITH CHANGE AGENTS

GOAL: ENABLING THE CATALYSTS OF CHANGE.

SEE THIS TOOL IN ACTION:
PAGE 55

Change. You can fight it and fail or embrace it and flourish.

Change agents are pathfinders who move us forward. They are the ones who recognize the future and know how to get there. Find the change agents in your organization and get them on board.

Change agents have the vision and skills to create a new "social architecture" as the basis of your organization's network.

Put a change agent on your design team. Change agents see the enterprise in terms of assets to be leveraged. When it comes to the design of new environments, they see opportunities to change work patterns and behaviors and to link new business processes and systems with facilities.

Since change agents often occupy the "in between" space within an enterprise, they see the world from a unique perspective. Harness their insights and possibilities will multiply.

Change agents focus less on specific goals and more on organizational readiness. Rather than aiming for straightforward growth, change agents aim for agility.

07

CREATE CHAMPIONS FOR THE VISION

GOAL: DEVELOPING A CRITICAL MASS OF SUPPORT FOR CHANGE.

SEE THIS TOOL IN ACTION:
PAGE 37

It's hard to realize a vision by yourself. It requires a critical mass of dedicated leaders at all levels within an enterprise. They must work across disciplinary boundaries to help people realize that the change required to achieve a vision is worth it.

Change is constant and often difficult. Change happens from the inside out, and from the outside in. It often requires behavioral change. Vision gives us inspiration and hope.

Identify key opinion leaders in the organization who support your enterprise vision and put them inside the change process. They'll help to spread the word. Their actions will foster an appropriate balance between vision and the daily activities required to get us there. As role models for those who follow, they play an important role in successfully launching a new paradigm and realizing a vision.

CATEGORY: COLLABORATION

DESIGN THE RELATIONSHIP

GOAL: HUMAN-CENTERED DESIGN BEGINS WITH HUMAN RELATIONSHIPS.

SEE THIS TOOL IN ACTION:
PAGE 112

It's a long ride. Know who you're driving with before you hit the road.

Before you begin the business of designing places, processes, and human experiences, start with each other. Articulate and understand personal and organizational values. Discover preferences for communication.

Before designing an environment, begin by designing the relationships with critical constituencies. Go beyond mirroring seniority levels to understand how to engage most effectively, both individually and collectively.

Understanding one another as people, knowing what we fundamentally value, enables us to move past the transactional. It frees us to address what is transformational. The environments we invest in are no longer mere commodities, but express deeply rooted aspirations.

How do you design the relationship? There are many ways. Focused Site Seeing builds relationships while deepening relevant knowledge. Off-site team-building retreats scheduled at the beginning of a project and at key milestones throughout the process build relationships and ensure that time for relationship building is a continuing priority.

Asking a physician why he originally went into medicine moves the conversation past the necessary and expected questions of medical delivery to questions of root cause. It reveals a fundamental belief in the healing power of nature and the design responds by integrating garden spaces throughout a medical environment.

Insights like this change our understanding of how the design of environments can inspire and transform us.

CATEGORY: COLLABORATION

WALK A MILE IN THEIR SHOES

GOAL: KNOWING YOUR CLIENT BY LIVING THE PROBLEM.

SEE THIS TOOL IN ACTION:
PAGE 120

Try walking in someone else's shoes. You'll gain insight while building empathy.

The best way to meet your client's needs is to get to know them really well. Spend as much time as you can with people who will use and live next to the buildings you are designing. Look for evidence of people's activities in their existing environments—where do they hang out, how do they organize their space, which places go unused?

Achieving an immersive, first-hand understanding of work patterns, habits, rituals, and movements helps clarify and prioritize client enterprise strategies prior to design. This indicates where behavioral change will need to be managed and sets the framework for performance-based design.

CATEGORY: COLLABORATION

INVEST IN TRAVEL

GOAL: BROADENING PERSPECTIVES.

SEE THIS TOOL IN ACTION:
PAGES 93, 148

Pack your bags and hit the road.

Become anthropologists. Together. Explore the way others inside and outside your field innovate with their processes and environments — even if it requires travel to a faraway country.

By taking field trips, you gain social proof that can be leveraged in support of new ideas. Look for examples of solutions that have worked in parallel situations. Study people's activities in these environments and note the relationship between places and activities.

Discuss how the environments you visit impact people's work lives, habits, and values. Talk to the people least likely to be asked their opinion. Document vigorously.

The journey provides context and background research for shared discovery, leading to the development of a project's vision. It helps connect everyone to a common experience that binds a team together.

CATEGORY: COLLABORATION

MAKE EVERYONE THE ARCHITECT

GOAL: ENSURING THAT THE BEST IDEA WINS.

SEE THIS TOOL IN ACTION:
PAGES 32, 63

You never know who will have the best idea. So ask.

Invite people to the table who aren't typically involved in design — people from a diverse range of activities within your enterprise whose experiences enable a broader understanding of behavior and flow. Including them at the design table allows their insights to have a direct impact on idea generation. Let a receptionist design the waiting areas. Ask transporters to design the corridor system. Invite hospital inpatients to design their room and the gowns they'll wear. Their solutions will both surprise and amaze you.

There are hidden experts waiting to get involved. When asked, they deliver real value.

CATEGORY: COLLABORATION

BREAK BREAD

GOAL: BUILDING TRUST AND COMMON UNDERSTANDING.

SEE THIS TOOL IN ACTION:
PAGE 118

Turn off the meter and pull over for a bite to eat.

Shed the trappings of professionalism—the client/consultant divide—and meet as people.

Changing the context for communication brings out diverse viewpoints that otherwise are left unsaid and thus unheard. Sharing a meal—away from the typical meeting structure—allows behavior to relax and perspectives to shift. When people sit and eat with each other they learn about life and each other, and build common ground.

The civilizing influence of that most basic of social structures, the meal, builds bridges and creates social networks that carry you forward. And when the inevitable difficult moments arise, the bonds and common understanding built in this simple but effective way help bring people together to resolve their differences.

CATEGORY: COLLABORATION

BUILD RENAISSANCE TEAMS

GOAL: INTEGRATING DIVERSE INTELLIGENCE YIELDS GREATER OPPORTUNITY FOR HIGH-PERFORMANCE OUTCOMES.

SEE THIS TOOL IN ACTION:
PAGE 173

Socrates was right. Dialogue is always more productive.

Given the sheer amount of and ready access to data and information in today's world it is no longer possible to be a Renaissance man or woman. So, rather than looking for the solitary genius, build Renaissance teams.

The most enlightened ideas start with the coming together of diverse perspectives. Include people who are broad and generous in their desire to work with others while having a depth of individual talent that adds color and breadth to your team. By integrating a variety of fully engaged talent from the start, you increase your chances of producing high-performance outcomes with lasting meaning.

Like-minded people have a tendency to develop like-minded solutions. This can lead to blind spots in process, ideation, and delivery. Renaissance teams help us individually break through the barriers of our training and ingrained processes.

When confronted with complex challenges, Renaissance teams see the challenges through multiple lenses. That increases their opportunity to develop a wider range of ideas with greater density of thought and action.

GIVE CLIENTS THE KEYS

GOAL: BEING OPEN TO AND SOLICITING ALTERNATIVE POINTS OF VIEW.

SEE THIS TOOL IN ACTION:
PAGE 169

Move over and let someone else drive. There's nothing like the view from the driver's seat to help clarify where you're going.

Give clients the metaphorical keys to your car and let them know they're welcome to drive any time. Invite them into your process. Expose them to your tools and teach their use. Make it clear from the beginning that the solution is just as likely to come from them as it is from you, especially when shifting to a new paradigm.

When clients are co-designers everyone owns the results, and the benefits to the larger enterprise are explicit.

CATEGORY: COMMUNICATION

MODEL IT

GOAL: VISUALIZING, UNDERSTANDING, AND COORDINATING.

SEE THIS TOOL IN ACTION:
PAGES 11, 157

Before you put the shovel in the ground, make sure everyone understands what it is they are getting. This upfront investment will provide a huge payback later, when ribbons are cut.

Two-dimensional drawings are a useful shorthand for planning and construction. However, while most building design professionals are educated to understand the abstraction of this form of graphic communication, the people they serve are not. Most clients have a difficult time fully understanding two-dimensional, drawings and are often reluctant to admit it.

Instead, make the communication of ideas and concepts three-dimensional like the world we live in. Use models at all scales to allow people to better imagine, experience, and test the comi reality. Tune the use of models to suit their role as communication, change management, or construction delivery tools. This helps you to arrive at the rig solution and save money in the long ru

IDEA MODELS

Rough idea models allow teams to test ideas rapidly. Idea models make the intangible tangible. Palm-sized idea models printed from a 3D printer can k used by teams who need to share concepts on the go. Use these quick studie to develop, test, and critique ideas.

LL-SCALE PROTOTYPES

l-scale rough prototypes of compli-
ted environments let people get inside,
on experiences, and "kick the tires."
beyond plywood and foam core; design
prototype to simulate not just spatial
eriences, but sensory experiences as
ll, such as light, aesthetics, and
ustics. Rigorously observe and record
w people use the environment, manip-
te elements, and interact with one
other when they are in the prototypes.

LL-SCALE MOCK-UPS

l-scale mock-ups differ from proto-
es since their primary use is as a
thful replica of a completed design
the testing of fit and finish during
struction. Mock-ups typically confirm
ality expectations and test our
derstanding of what is to be built.

IMMERSIVE 4D MODELS

When large shifts in the way people work
are expected for a move into a new
building, use immersive 4D models as
powerful change management tools. For
large groups, real-time models shown in
IMAX-type theater settings offer the
closest parallel to physical space. The
ability to take employees or members of
the public on a "walk-through" builds
understanding. Because a 4D model sim-
ulates experience, it breeds familiarity,
helps eradicate unknowns, and manages
the resistance to change.

BUILDING INFORMATION MODELING

Designers and builders now offer new
delivery solutions that address the
unpredictability and adversarial nature
of the traditional design-bid-build
process. Building Information Modeling
(BIM) creates intelligent digital 3D
models instead of paper drawings to
communicate design ideas, and guide
construction. BIM creates an integrated
solution with fewer elements of risk for
all parties. Taken to the next level,
Building Information Modeling will move
toward "Enterprise Information
Modeling," where data captured during
programming and pre-design will allow
for strategic scenario development as it
impacts the built environment.

SPEAK THE RIGHT LANGUAGE

GOAL: LEARNING THE CLIENT'S LANGUAGE.

SEE THIS TOOL IN ACTION:
PAGE 153

Eschew obfuscation! Leave the jargon at home and learn the language of your client's enterprise.

Every client, industry, or organization has a way of communicating that's all its own. Figure out what those "languages" are. Develop a common language that is comfortable and productive—words, charts, diagrams, images, models, objects.... Sometimes, it can even be places or body language. Don't rely on just one language. Being multilingual means you'll have a greater opportunity to communicate and understand.

Early in the design process, as a means of understanding the client's enterprise, ask participants to create a collage that explains a particular process or experience that they feel is important to their enterprise. Have them explain the significance of images chosen. Associating descriptions with different design concepts or features helps people verbalize complex themes. It helps the team evaluate and prioritize design features and concepts. It builds shared understanding and shapes the language of design intent.

When communicating design concepts, explore the use of different "languages" to ensure that people understand the connection between their enterprise and the design. Learn what "language" makes your client most comfortable and use it when you're with them.

CATEGORY: COMMUNICATION

DESIGN ON THE FLY

GOAL: VISUALIZING AND UNDER-STANDING IDEAS IN REAL TIME.

SEE THIS TOOL IN ACTION:
PAGE 97

Transcend words. Stop mid-sentence and express an idea visually, right now. You'll be surprised how quickly people really understand what you mean.

Draw, sketch, diagram, and map ideas in real time; involve everyone, not just the designers. Think of problem-solving in hallways, cafes, and mid-meeting as just-in-time design.

When team members talk about ideas and concepts, make it visual on the spot. Everyone can then ask: "Is this what you mean?" for a quick joint grasp of intent.

Real-time sketching resolves problems the moment they occur. It allows the team to rapidly explore, articulate, and visualize design concepts. Sometimes they are simple studies that explore causality—if you want x, it means redesigning y. Other times, they test behaviors—if you're going to work like this in the new environment, it looks like that. Accelerated explorations surface the key aspects of an issue as it relates to the built environment. They move conversations from the abstract to a tangible visual expression of an idea—from problem to solution.

CATEGORY: DELIVERY

DESIGN THE PROCESS

GOAL: CREATING PROCESS CLARITY AND A ROAD MAP FOR REALIZING YOUR VISION.

SEE THIS TOOL IN ACTION:
PAGES 83, 141

What's the issue? Who's responsible? By when? Let the people involved determine the answers.

Every client challenge, site, and context is unique. That's why it's just as important to design the process for a project as it is to design the project. Managing a creative course of action means building methods and tools that help people collaborate around a shared vision.

Change projects are big, complex journeys into uncharted territory. You need a road map that identifies key milestones. They will keep you on course, guiding your efforts while giving you the freedom to make course corrections along the way.

JAZZ THE PROCESS

We're not just reading sheet music here.

Rather than writing down every note, jazz creates a collectively understood and agreed upon creative framework. It sets themes that allow for and encourage individual variation. Rather than being entirely prescriptive, jazz is a guide, a compass for creativity that anticipates change and adaptability. Jazz acknowledges the reality of constantly changing circumstances and builds in the ability to make adjustments while staying on course.

Design the design process as if you are a jazz ensemble.

There is clearly an element of trust in jazz. A musical framework points everyone in the same direction and creates touchstones that allow the ensemble to monitor their progress. Within this

...ategic framework, individuals are
...en a range of freedom to chart their
...n courses, trusting in each other's
...ent.

...a symphony all eyes are on the
...nductor. In jazz, all eyes and ears are
...each other—watchful, vigilant, ready
...change and willing to adapt as the
...expected occurs.

...ILD TOUCHSTONES

...learly worded mission statement,
...hort set of guiding principles, story-
...ards that combine text and images
...visually communicate vision, concept,
...d progress—keep them handy to use
...enever decisions come up. They keep
...r vision accessible, reminding you
...where you began and where you
...going.

HOLD REGULARLY SCHEDULED MEETINGS TO CONSTANTLY DESIGN THE PROCESS

Hold a session to initiate the design of the ideal process for the project based on your organization, the key stakeholders, and the vision. Inspired minds alone, however prolific, are nothing without processes designed specifically to translate ideas into valuable solutions. Anticipate change by scheduling periodic meetings. Use them to review, update, and change the process to meet changing needs and conditions.

DEFINE EVERYONE'S ROLE

Put everyone's title in a drawer and instead focus on the clarity of each person's role. Assess team talent, interest and passion to determine who should be responsible for what.

Initiate a meeting to define who owns what. Ask each person to state his or her interests. Then ask each person to state what he or she expects from others—clients, user advocates, architects, engineers, contractors. Explore the intriguing area of expectation that lies outside your own view of what you're "supposed" to do.

The passion, intelligence, and persistence of a large team of people made this book, and the work it contains, possible. The *Change Design* editorial team is grateful to the following people who helped bring this book into realization.

CHANGE CONVERSATIONS
JON FREDRIK BAKSAAS, President/CEO, Telenor; SUSAN DORIA, Senior Vice President, Strategic Development, Banner Health; CAROLYN CORVI, Vice President/General Manager, Airplane Production, Boeing Commercial Airplanes, The Boeing Company; JIM REED, Acting Director of Fiscal Policy, Washington State Higher Education Coordinating Board; JOHN COOPER, Director of Resources, Wellcome Trust Sanger Institute; ALLAN BRADLEY, Director, Wellcome Trust Sanger Institute; PHIL BUTCHER, Head of Information Technology, Wellcome Trust Sanger Institute; BRUCE RIFKIN, District Court Executive, United States District Court, Western District of Washington; JOHN C. COUGHENOUR, United States District Judge, Western District of Washington; LARRY SMARR, Director, California Institute for Telecommunications and Information Technology (Calit2).

We would also like to thank Dag Melgaard, Telenor; Jeff Nelson, Banner Estrella; Douglas Noonan, Reebok International Ltd.; Robin McBr and Craig Martin, The Boeing Company; Coke Putnam, HECB; and Stephanie Sides and Doug Ramsey, Calit2.

The Telenor project covered in this section was designed as a joint venture between NBBJ-HUS PKA. Banner Estrella was designed by NBBJ in partnership with Phoenix-based Orcutt Winslo Partnership.

TALKING POINTS
PAUL FIREMAN, Founder and former CEO; HOWA SCHULTZ, Chairman, Starbucks Corporation; KWEK LENG BENG, Executive Chairman, City Developments Limited; DR. TOBY COSGROVE, CEO/Chairman of the Board of Governors; DR. FLOYD LOOP, former CEO, The Cleveland

hic Foundation; ADA HEALEY, Vice President
Real Estate, Vulcan, Inc.

ANGE ESSAYS
NIEL PINK, author; JEANNE LIEDTKA,
cutive Director, Batten Institute, University
Virginia; RICHARD SWETT, author and Senior
ow, Design Futures Council; ALEXI MARMOT,
hor and founder, AMA Alexi Marmot
ociates; BRUCE MAU, founder and Creative
ector, Bruce Mau Design Inc.

ANGE TOOLS
ny staff members at NBBJ helped in capturing
characterizing the Change Tools: Cam Allen,
iam Bain, Friedrich Böhm, Blaine Brownell,
istian Carlson, Anne Cunningham,
tt Dunlap, Jay Halleran, Liz Jacks,
Johnson, Jim Jonassen, Michael Kreis,
d Leathley, Charles Martin, Steve McConnell,

AJ Montero, Bruce Nepp, Bill Nichols, JinAh Park,
Fred Powell, Peter Pran, Martin Regge, Brent
Rogers, Rysia Suchecka, Bill Sanford, James
Tully, Vince Vergel de Dios, Lori Walker, and
Jonathan Ward.

Thank you to Jim Cramer of Östberg Press and
The Greenway Group for his impeccable timing
and thoughtful publishing approach.

CHANGE DESIGN EDITORIAL TEAM
BRUCE MAU DESIGN INC.: Bruce Mau with
Angelica Fox, Interviewer, Writer and Editor;
Ian Rapsey, Designer; Kevin Sugden, Designer;
and Michael Waldin, Project Manager.

NBBJ: Scott Wyatt, Richard Dallam, and
Timothy Johnson with Helen Dimoff, Managing
Editor; Bonnie Duncan, Editorial; and
Andrea Jeanne Larsen, Photo Editor.

PHOTOGRAPHY & ILLUSTRATION
Assassi Productions, Dan Bibb, Craig Brookes,
Peter Cook, Alan Decker/NY Times, Scott Dunlap,
John Durant, Jeff Goldberg/Esto, Tim Griffith,
Robert Hood, Timothy Hursley, Andrea Jeanne
Larsen, Michelle Litvin, Steve McConnell,
Matt Milios, Frank Ooms, Don Powell, Publicis
Singapore, Christian Richters, Kim Selby, Sherry
Snow, Lara Swimmer, and Scott Wyatt.

WE LOOKED AT COURTHOUSES ACROSS THE COUNTRY—WONDERFUL BUILDINGS, EXTRAORDINARY ICONS—WHERE A COMMITMENT TO THE EXCELLENCE OF WHAT WAS INSIDE HAD BEEN LOST BECAUSE THE PERFORMANCE OF THE BUILDING HADN'T BEEN MADE A GOAL OF THE ARCHITECTURE.

BRUCE RIFKIN

WE WERE VERY DELIBERATE IN OUR CO-LOCATION EFFORTS IN ORDER TO BUILD A BUSINESS CULTURE AROUND THE CO-LOCATION EXERCISE.

JON FREDRIK BAKSAAS

I TOOK EVERYTHING I'VE LEARNED OVER THE YEARS AND TRIED TO TRANSFORM IT FROM BEING AN ODD THING THAT HAD HAPPENED TO SOMETHING THAT THE ARCHITECTURE WOULD MAKE MORE COMMON.

LARRY SMARR

CARDIAC SURGEONS NO LONGER HAVE MUCH IN COMMON WITH LIVER SURGEONS, BUT HAVE LOTS IN COMMON WITH CARDIAC ANESTHESIOLOGISTS. THIS NEW SPACE GIVES ME THE OPPORTUNITY TO REORGANIZE THE CLINIC AROUND ORGAN SYSTEMS.

DR. TOBY COSGROVE

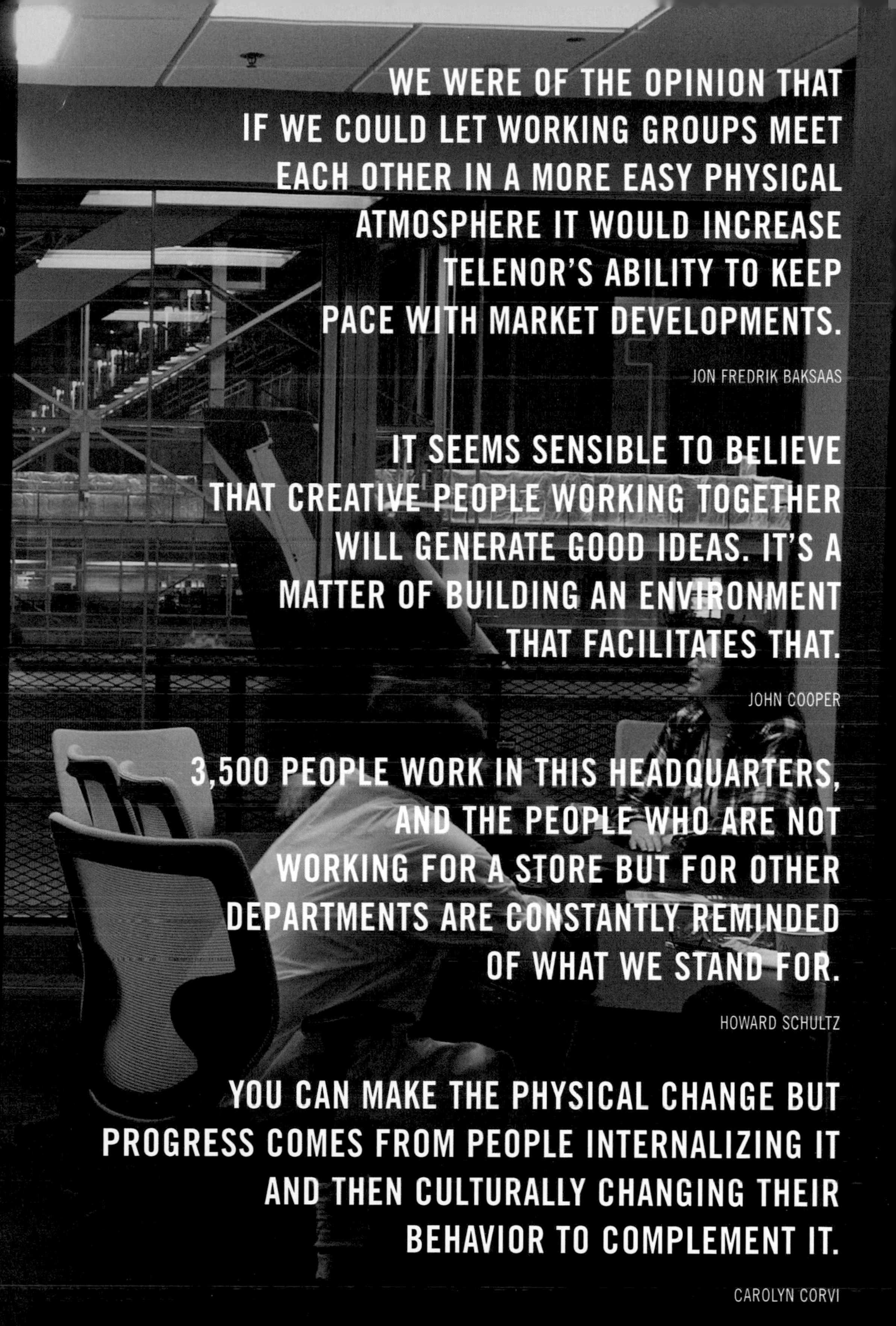

WE WERE OF THE OPINION THAT
IF WE COULD LET WORKING GROUPS MEET
EACH OTHER IN A MORE EASY PHYSICAL
ATMOSPHERE IT WOULD INCREASE
TELENOR'S ABILITY TO KEEP
PACE WITH MARKET DEVELOPMENTS.

JON FREDRIK BAKSAAS

IT SEEMS SENSIBLE TO BELIEVE
THAT CREATIVE PEOPLE WORKING TOGETHER
WILL GENERATE GOOD IDEAS. IT'S A
MATTER OF BUILDING AN ENVIRONMENT
THAT FACILITATES THAT.

JOHN COOPER

3,500 PEOPLE WORK IN THIS HEADQUARTERS,
AND THE PEOPLE WHO ARE NOT
WORKING FOR A STORE BUT FOR OTHER
DEPARTMENTS ARE CONSTANTLY REMINDED
OF WHAT WE STAND FOR.

HOWARD SCHULTZ

YOU CAN MAKE THE PHYSICAL CHANGE BUT
PROGRESS COMES FROM PEOPLE INTERNALIZING IT
AND THEN CULTURALLY CHANGING THEIR
BEHAVIOR TO COMPLEMENT IT.

CAROLYN CORVI

THE DESIGN OF THE BUILDING WAS THE MOST
FORMATIVE ASPECT OF CREATING CALIT2 BECAUSE IT
FORCED PEOPLE FROM DIFFERENT DISCIPLINES
TO COME TOGETHER, LISTEN TO EACH OTHER'S
OPINIONS, AND MAKE COLLECTIVE
DECISIONS. IT CREATED OUR CULTURAL DNA.

LARRY SMARR

WE BENCHMARK OURSELVES AGAINST OTHER PEER
ORGANIZATIONS AROUND THE COUNTRY, AND BANNER ESTRELLA
HOSPITAL IS HITTING THE 99TH PERCENTILE IN PATIENT
SATISFACTION. PEOPLE HAVE NEW TOOLS TO
PROVIDE BETTER CARE.

SUSAN DORIA

MANY PEOPLE SAY, "IT'S AMAZING.
OUR PRODUCTIVITY'S INCREASED SINCE WE'VE
MOVED IN." CONSIDERING ALL THE UPSET
CAUSED BY MOVING INTO A NEW BUILDING, IT'S
INTERESTING THAT PEOPLE ARE ALREADY
FEELING A POSITIVE IMPACT.

ALLAN BRADLEY

THE NEW HEADQUARTERS HAS CHANGED THE
WAY OUR PEOPLE THINK OF THE BUSINESS WHEN
THEY WAKE UP IN THE MORNING. YOU'RE LIVING
THE BRAND EXPERIENCE. I VIEW THIS
AS A RENAISSANCE.

PAUL FIREMAN